# BOATING, BIKING AND HIKING
## — THE —
# MONMOUTHSHIRE & BRECON CANAL

by Jennifer Petkus

Mallard Travel
Denver, Colorado

ISBN 13: 978-0-9995627-1-0
ISBN 10: 0-9995627-1-1

## Acknowledgments

*Many thanks to Jaymie James, whose panoramas of the Mon & Brec on Google Street View really helped me confirm details.*
*I hope you find your way home.*

*And to the many organizations—the Monmouthshire, Brecon & Abergavenny Canal Trust; the Canal & River Trust; and the Inland Waterways Association, to name just a few—that keep the canals alive and healthy, thank you.*

*And thanks to my proofreaders, including my best friend Lee Thomas; fellow narrowboater Brenda Ward; novice narrowboater Susan Whitaker; and Trevor J. Riches, who just volunteered in response to a facebook post. And to my husband, Jim Bates, who puts up with me.*

# Table of Contents

*Looking toward the Central Beacons of Brecon Beacons National Park near Llanfrynach*

# A trip on the Monmouthshire & Brecon Canal

I t's hard to imagine a more magical, beautiful and relaxing vacation than boating, biking or hiking the Monmouthshire & Brecon Canal in South Wales. The canal meanders through the Usk River Valley, hugging the sides of mountains, and progressing with stately ceremony through one picturesque town after another. On the way you'll be serenaded by the lowing of cows, the baas of sheep and the snorts of horses.

If you're very lucky, you might see the electric blue flash of a kingfisher. You're guaranteed to see a heron lazily watching your boat or a buzzard flying high overhead. Swans and ducks will be your constant companions. Should you leave the canal and follow the Usk, you might be rewarded with the sight of an otter or badger. If you're very, very lucky—and I mean win the lottery lucky—you might see a water vole returning to a hole along the banks of the canal or river.

At the steady putt-putt of your narrowboat, the measured tread of your feet or the rhythm of your wheels, you'll experience life, nature, friendships and your own thoughts in a way few of us can enjoy in daily life. On a narrowboat, you'll find it difficult to exceed two and a half miles an hour. As a hiker, you'll easily slow to talk with narrowboat crews—passing pleasantries or suggestions of where to eat—and then resume your pace to quickly leave the boat behind.

On a bike you might achieve a heady six miles an hour, but your effective speed will be much less because you'll be constantly stopping to take pictures, sample blackberries or tour a castle a mile or two from the canal.

It's true that you could ruin a trip on the Mon & Brec by not discarding the baggage of daily life. You could chafe at the speed of your journey, the pace of country life or the intermittent cellular service. If you're on a narrowboat, you might curse every time your boat runs aground. If you've been walking for hours and finally reached a welcoming pub, only to be told they just finished lunch or dinner service, you might grumble. On a bike, you might shudder at the thought of a rainy ride down a muddy towpath.

My only advice is to let the sound of water rushing into a lock wash away your insistence that everything goes your way. It will rain on your trip, the village post office will close at 2 pm and in times of drought the locks close at 6 pm.

Fortunately canal travelers are self-selecting. If you appreciate the more than 200 years of history the canal represents; if you find yourself humming *Men of Harlech* while visiting the Regimental Museum of the Royal Welsh[1]; if you don't mind squatting on the towpath in the rain, camera up to your eye, waiting for a heron to look your way; then you should definitely travel the Mon & Brec, whether by narrowboat, kayak, canoe, paddleboard, bicycle or on foot.

## A few notes about this guide

This book is intended as a guide to the still navigable portion of the Mon & Brec, the 35mi/56.3km stretch from Brecon to Pontypool. The idea for this guide came about after a 2018 narrowboat trip on the canal. Although we were armed with the informative and useful **The**

---

[1]    Watch the 1964 movie *Zulu* starring Stanley Baker and Michael Caine if you miss this reference

**Mon and Brec Guide**  edited by Phil Hughes, I thought I'd take a crack at writing one. Mr. Hughes' guide is exhaustive in its detail, and if you see anything on the canal and wonder what it is, his guide will undoubtedly tell you. But I thought I might add the perspective of a reasonably well informed American with a penchant for cycling and hiking.

This guide is not meant to be a primer on how to handle a narrowboat. For that I have written **Narrowboating for Beginners: What Americans need to know when considering a narrowboat vacation in the UK** . In that book you'll find out how to turn a lock, steer the boat and moor.

This guide *will* show you every bridge, lock, aqueduct, waterpoint and mooring on the canal, and list most of the attractions, services, hotels, inns and B&Bs as well. Obviously I have not visited every hotel, inn and B&B on the canal so my listings are unrated.

You'll find some paragraphs marked with icons, which represents tips, information and warnings. You'll also see throughout the book **Text in bold** followed by . This indicates there is a corresponding QR code and shortened url at the end of that chapter. You can use your tablet or smartphone to scan the code and open a resource on the internet. Or, just type in the shortened bit.ly address into your web browser.

 The Mon &
Brec Guide
`bit.ly/2WABhZr`

Narrowboating
for Beginners (US)
`amzn.to/2WpUvMp`

 Narrowboating
for Beginners (UK)
`amzn.to/2WZJQMt`

*The canals are used for so many activities. Above, cyclists aided by electric motors can easily travel the length of the canal in a day. Below, locals can wave at narrowboaters while relaxing with their dogs on the towpath.*

*The River Usk, the source of the Mon & Brec Canal*

# The Vale of Usk

## The Route

The Monmouthshire & Brecon Canal is born in Brecon where it's fed by the 74.6mi/120km River Usk. The supply from the river starts at a weir about a third of a mile (500m) northwest of the bridge over the Usk in Brecon, as shown above. One can easily walk to the weir via the Promenade walk *(see page 32)* that follows the eastern bank of the river. The water is diverted under the town and discharges into the canal basin that is the terminus (end) of the canal.

The canal follows a southeasterly route, hugging the edges of the Usk Valley[1] and is almost completely within the confines of Brecon Beacons National Park. From Brecon heading south, you have spectacular views of the Central Beacons[2] looking to the west and the Black

---

1    Less scenically, the canal is close to the A40, which runs along the northern edge of the national park, around Brecon and then to Abergavenny. The A40 heads east near Llanellen and continues to Monmouth and then up through the Wye Valley. Fortunately you'll rarely notice the A40 from the canal.

2    I've yet to find a definitive reference, but many books suggest the Brecon Beacons are so-called because fires were once lit on mountaintops to warn of invading forces. Because of the visibility of peaks like Pen-y-Fan, it makes sense that there would be a long history of using the beacons to transmit messages. Iron Age tribes may have used the beacons to warn of attacks from other tribes; the

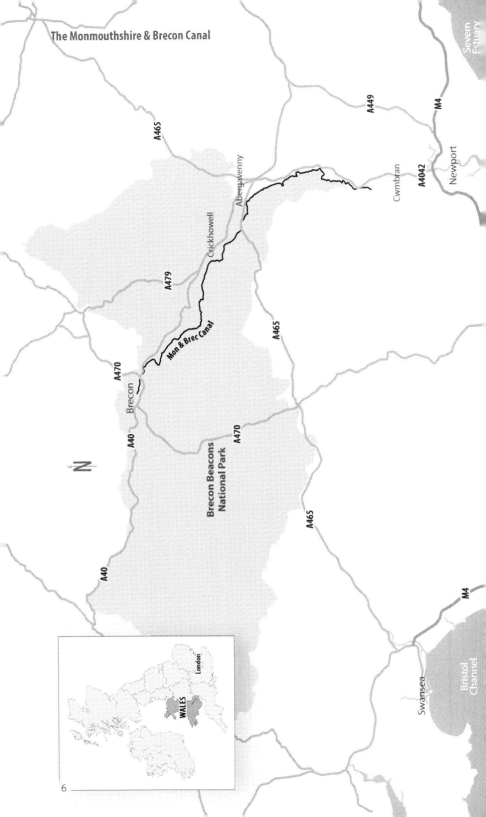

# The Monmouthshire & Brecon Canal

Severn Estuary

A449

M4

Newport

Cwmbran

A4042

Abergavenny

A465

Crickhowell

A479

A465

Mon & Brec Canal

A470

Brecon

A40

A470

Brecon Beacons National Park

A465

N

A40

M4

Swansea

Bristol Channel

London

WALES

Mountains looking east. Near Abergavenny you'll have views of Sugar Loaf mountain to the north and The Blorenge to the south.

Villages and towns along the canal include Brecon, Llanfrynach, Talybont-on-Usk, Llangynidr, Llangattock, Crickhowell, Gilwern, Govilon, Llanfoist, Abergavenny and Penperlleni. After 21 miles near the village of Llanellen, the canal heads south while the Usk continues east.

The length of the navigable portion of the canal is about 35mi/56.3km, but many would argue just how much of the present-day canal is navigable. The Canal & River Trust, the UK charity that owns and operates 2,000mi/3,200km of navigable waterways in the UK, controls the canal from Brecon in the north to Bridge 47 in Sebastopol[3] (a suburb of Pontypool and north of Cwmbran) in the south. Realistically, few narrowboats go much further south than Goytre Wharf or Pontymoile (another suburb of Pontypool) Basin because the canal is increasingly choked with vegetation as you travel south.

The canal does continue south of Bridge 47 and theoretically a narrowboat could travel another three-quarters of a mile (1.2km) to where the canal disappears underground just north of Five Locks Road. However the replacement of the Bevans Lane Bridge[4] has done much to further exacerbate the weed growth in this final navigable section.

Because the canal mostly follows the contours of the surrounding hills and mountains, there are only six locks dropping a mere 60ft/18.3m. South from the Llangynidr flight of five locks, boaters can enjoy 23 lock-free miles (37km).

## Lost route to the Severn Estuary

Narrowboats cannot proceed past Five Locks Road in Cwmbran but the canal does continue south toward Newport in piecemeal fashion. It often disappears under intersections and roundabouts and finally ends rather sadly at a roundabout where the M4 crosses the A4051. In fact if you're negotiating the roundabout there you might catch a quick

---

Welsh may have used them to warn of Roman attacks, and vice versa; or the simplest explanation, the Welsh may have used the beacons to signal the approach of the English forces of Edward I. The beacons were also used to celebrate the Golden and Diamond Jubilees of Queen Victoria, the formation of the European Union and the millennium celebrations in 2000.

3    Named after the city of Sevastopol on the Black Sea which Great Britain and its allies captured in 1855 during the Crimean War

4    That work was scheduled to complete by June 2019 after which narrowboats should once again be able to travel to Five Locks Basin

glimpse of water behind low brick walls. Actually don't look; it's a very sad sight.

The towpath on the abandoned section of the canal, however, makes a very good cycling and walking route. The towpath is also part of National Cycle Route 49 *(see page 20)*.

### Crumlin Arm

The Monmouthshire Canal *(see History below)* was originally only 12.5mi/20.1km long, but the Crumlin Arm added another 11mi/18km. Unfortunately what was the beginning of the canal at Crumlin is lost under the A467, but it reappears at Cwmcarn and then continues southeast to the Cefn flight of fourteen locks. The arm dips under the M4 before joining the main route of the Mon & Brec near the roundabout mentioned previously.

## History

As with most canals, the Monmouthshire & Brecon Canal has a complicated history of enthusiasm, speculation, competition from the railways, neglect, restoration and unfulfilled promise. The modern-day canal is a combination of two canals, the Monmouthshire and the Brecknock & Abergavenny. An Act of Parliament authorized the first canal in 1792, the second in 1793.

The Brecknock & Abergavenny ran, unsurprisingly, from Brecon to Abergavenny. The Monmouthshire, meanwhile, was a connection from Pontnewynydd to Newport and via the River Usk to the Bristol Channel and the Severn. The two canals met in 1812 at Pontymoile.[5] Of the modern-day canal's current 35-mile length, less than two miles of the original course of the Monmouthshire are included in the modern-day Mon & Brec.

The canals were principally created as connections to the many tramways that fed coal, limestone and iron ore to the rest of Wales and Britain. The tramways were simple rails on which horses pulled ore carts, although over time they formed the basis of a number of true railways.

The railways, of course, spelled the doom of the Mon & Brec. The Monmouthshire Canal Company, relabeled the Monmouthshire Railway and Canal Company, bought the Brecknock & Abergavenny Canal in 1865. By 1880 the canals were under the ownership of the Great Western Railway. Soon the railway all but abandoned the Monmouthshire Canal with the Brecknock & Abergavenny existing

---

5   The Mon & Brec celebrated its 200th anniversary in 2012

primarily as water supply to the Newport Docks. The Crumlin Arm, however, survived as a commercial waterway until the 1930s. The canals were formally abandoned in 1962.

## Restoration

Efforts to save the canals began even before formal closure with an Inland Waterways Association rally in 1952 in Brecon and active restoration began just a few years after abandonment. The canal was reopened from Brecon to Pontymoile in 1970 and restoration of the original Monmouthshire Canal began in 1994. The Crumlin Arm has also seen new locks installed, but unfortunately fully restoring the canal from Brecon to Newport remains a daunting task. The Canal & River Trust only owns the currently navigable two miles of what was the Monmouthshire Canal. The rest of the Monmouthshire Canal including the Crumlin Arm is under the control of various entities, including the Caerphilly Borough County Council, the Torfaen Borough County Council and the Newport City Council.

In 2018 the CRT announced a proposed £65 million restoration effort that would make navigable the Mon & Brec past Five Locks Road all the way to the now abandoned Barrack Hill tunnel, possibly all the way to the Usk. In addition to the previously named entities, this plan would also need the cooperation of the Monmouthshire, Brecon and Abergavenny Canals Trust and the Brecon Beacons National Park Authority.

## "A popular place to be alone"

The character of the Monmouthshire & Brecon Canal is strongly influenced by being an isolated canal—not connected to the rest of the canal network. In theory one could travel by narrowboat from Lancaster to London on canals and navigable rivers, but the only way to get a narrowboat to the Mon & Brec is to haul it there by lorry. In fact the overwhelming majority of boats on the Mon & Brec were purpose built for the canal.

 Although at first glance most Mon & Brec narrowboats look like their counterparts elsewhere on the canal network, they are different. None are more than 60 feet long, but they can be up to 9 feet wide. Because the Mon & Brec is a notoriously shallow canal, most boats are also designed with a shallow draft.

Another influence on the character is the fact that most of the narrowboats on the canal are hire boats. There are few residential moorings on the Mon & Brec, meaning you can't live on your boat in one spot year round. The consequence of this is that many of the boaters on the canal are visitors and many are first-time boaters.

There's a certain camaraderie as a consequence and you'll spend a lot of time talking with other boaters. Most of the hikers and cyclists are similarly tourists enjoying the Brecon Beacons. Every hotel, pub and bed and breakfast on the canal also go out of their way to cater to boaters, cyclists and walkers.

The few locks and lift bridges on the canal also contribute to a relaxed atmosphere, as well as the unofficial but wisely observed 2½ mph speed limit on narrowboats. At that speed, necessary because of the shallow canal, it's difficult to get into too much trouble.

Despite the canal's popularity, there are many stretches of the canal where you won't encounter another boat, cyclist or walker. And yet it takes only a little effort to walk to a pub or country store. Paradoxically the Mon & Brec is a popular place to be alone.

*Looking up Cross Street in Abergavenny toward the market clock tower*

*Weeds make it nearly impossible, especially for a novice boater, to travel south from Goytre Wharf on the Monmouthshire & Brecon Canal*

# Challenges & Resources

Even though the Monmouthshire & Brecon Canal is beautiful and will probably be one of the best vacations of your life, it does present some challenges. In consolation, however, those challenges are often related to what makes the canal so unique.

## Common challenges

### Getting there

If you don't live in the UK, getting to the canal isn't easy. You can't fly to the nearest airports, Cardiff or Bristol, from the US without considerable expense and multiple stops or airlines. It makes the most sense to fly to London or Manchester and either rent a car or take a train to the canal.

*Train service*

Unfortunately the only train service to the canal is at Abergavenny and there are no narrowboat hire companies based there, however some of the hire companies will pick you up at the train station. You can book your rail trip at the **National Rail Journey Planner** Ⓦ.

*Taxis and buses*

Fortunately there are numerous private taxi companies (a bloke with a car) convenient to the canal and there are ride sharing services like Uber. There is bus service along the Usk Valley and you can plan your trip at **Traveline** . Bus route 43 or X43 goes from Brecon to Abergavenny closely following the canal and Hereford-Cardiff route X3 goes from Abergavenny to Newport following the A4042. The buses are operated by Stagecoach South Wales. Unfortunately the ability to bring a bike, other than a fold-up one, on a bus is unpredictable.

> Although I've listed several taxi services, the best way to find a taxi once you're in Wales is to ask for a recommendation at a pub. You'll probably get a tour guide *and* transportation for one price.

*Rental car*

There are car hire companies in Brecon, Newport and Cwmbran and generally boat hire companies will allow you to park a car at their location for the length of your trip. On our 2018 trip, we flew into London Heathrow, took a train to Bristol and from there drove a rented car to our boat hire. After our canal trip we used the rental car to tour the Brecon Beacons.

## The River Usk

The River Usk, responsible for so much of the charm and even the existence of the canal, also makes getting around a little difficult. As does the A40, which parallels the river and the canal. Often the pub or attraction you wish to visit will be on the other side of the River Usk, and there's no convenient bridge, especially on foot, to cross it. Cyclists have a big advantage in being able to ride a mile or two from the canal to find an out of the way pub or restaurant.

The terrain of the Usk Valley also imposes some difficulties. The canal is usually higher than the villages and towns, so you'll find that little walk to the pub or store involves more elevation change than you'd bargained for. Good walking shoes are a must.

## Cell reception/TV signal/Internet access

Cell reception is actually pretty decent and is best where the canal is closest to the A40 or A465. Nevertheless, depending on where you moor you may find little or no signal. You can check coverage at **OpenSignal** .

Even though your narrowboat probably comes with a TV and antenna, you'll probably only enjoy reception near Brecon and Abergavenny.

Remember to remove the antenna whenever going through the Ashford Tunnel and the many low bridges on the canal. In fact it's probably best to remove the antenna whenever the boat is moving.

Your narrowboat hire may or not offer on board Wi-Fi and, of course, it's still dependent on cellular service. Most pubs, inns and B&Bs have in-room Wi-Fi. Some campgrounds may offer Wi-Fi and charging stations in a common area.

## Dining

Dining can be an unexpected challenge, whether you're boating, cycling or hiking. A quick glance at Google Maps will show a number of pubs along the Mon & Brec, but your plans and their food service hours are often at odds. Most pubs offer lunch service from noon to 2 pm and dinner service from 6 to 9 pm. Many pubs are also closed on Mondays (or some other random day of the week) and often you'll arrive at a pub, tired and hungry, and see a sign saying "No food service today," even though you checked the pub's website or called ahead. Good help is hard to find and when it doesn't show up, there's no one to cook or serve.

 Even if you don't plan to cook on a narrowboat, it's best to stock up on basic supplies to get you through a night without dinner. Cyclists and hikers should at least have trail mix as consolation for a missed meal. Fortunately there are frequent water points along the towpath.

*Etiquette*

If it looks like a pub, just find a table you like, note the table number and go to the bar to order food. Attempting anything else will just confuse the pub staff. You only need tip if service was exceptional. If you're at a restaurant where you were seated, tip as you see fit, probably in the 10–15 percent range. Your check, however, may already include a suggested tip.

## Parking

Parking in the towns and villages along the canal is best accomplished in self-service parking lots. Surprising to many American visitors, even grocery store car parks are paid. (You might even have to rent a shopping trolley/cart, but you'll be reimbursed when you return it.) In many cases, however, overnight parking is free.

Be wary when a hotel you've booked indicates on its website that parking is available—it may only mean that a car park is nearby.

Cars parked facing different directions on the same side of a street may confuse you. It's permitted to park opposite the direction of traffic on streets with a speed limit of 30 mph or under.

## Speed limits

 Something that's very confusing to Americans is the lack of speed limit signs on many roadways. You might overlook a sign that simply looks like a "Don't do this" warning without indicating what you're not supposed to do. This sign actually indicates you should follow the national speed limit for the type of road you're on. Tourists to the UK who plan to drive should read the **UK Highway Code** ⓘ. Oh, and by the way, the speed limit signs are in miles per hour. You'd also be advised to watch videos on how to **negotiate a roundabout** ⓘ. Although they're less frequent in the country-side you will still encounter them.

## Weather

Wales, of course, is notorious for wet weather. Although narrowboats are usually equipped with one waterproof jacket, anyone visiting Wales should prepare to be wet. Assume at least half your time on the canal will be spent in the rain (although I was wet only a quarter of the time during my September trip).

## Dogs

Most narrowboat hires allow dogs on board although there are differing restrictions. And because so many people travel with their dogs on holiday, you'll notice that most pubs are very dog friendly. Hotels often include a surcharge for pets.

# Boating challenges

The main challenge to narrowboating on the canal is its shallowness. You'll know the canal is too shallow when your boat emits an unholy keening, wailing, grating sound. If you're a novice boater, you'll think you've done something wrong when you suddenly can't move the boat forward or back. It's undoubtedly caught on sand or silt and you'll have to use the boat's pole to free it. Sticking to the deeper middle of the canal will help, but when passing another boat you'll have to move closer to the bank. Silt deposits more easily in slower water, so you'll find the canal shallower on the inside of bends and on the "upstream" side of bridges.

If pushing the throttle forward or in reverse seems to have no effect, cut the throttle, count to ten and try again but slower. Sometimes in shallow water the prop sucks the boat tight to the canal bottom. Cutting the throttle allows the water to settle and the boat to rise.

A consequence of the shallowness (and narrowness) of the Mon & Brec means you should obey the unofficial speed limit[1] of 2–2½ mph. Most canals have an official speed limit of 4 mph, but in reality you should never travel so fast that your boat's wake leaves a breaking wash along the canal bank. This erodes the bank and in some areas might even lead to a catastrophic canal breach. Unfortunately the Monmouthshire & Brecon Canal leaks like a sieve and several embankments have slipped or breached over the years, the most significant recently in October 2007 near Gilwern. Three houses were damaged and eight people were rescued from the floodwaters.

 How fast are you traveling? After all, narrowboats don't have speedometers, but at 2½ mph, people walking on the towpath, even carrying backpacks, will easily out pace your boat. You can also install a speedometer app on your GPS-enabled phone or tablet.

Another challenge is the low clearance under many bridges and in the Ashford Tunnel. You'll probably be advised to keep your water tank topped to make the boat have a deeper draft and thus avoid scraping the top of the tunnel. Unfortunately this will also make your boat more likely to get caught on the bottom.

Of course in 2018 many parts of the UK had reduced rainfall. On the Mon & Brec, as a consequence, the six locks on the canal were locked between 6 pm and 10 am. This ensures both more water for downstream consumers of the River Usk and adequate canal levels, but these restrictions require boaters to plan ahead.

 You will want to download from the Canal & River Trust a **current boater's guide** 🕸 just before your trip to see what restrictions are in effect. Fortunately most canal closures (for regular repairs) occur in the winter months. You can also subscribe to be regularly notified by email of any **stoppages or restrictions** 🕸 on any canal.

## Returning

All the locks are on the northern third of the canal, however the various hire boat companies are strung out along its length. Boat hires

---

1    I have yet to find an official CRT statement about a speed limit on the Mon & Brec

*A folding bike can easily fit in the well deck at the front of the boat*

want you to return the boat early on your last rental day, typically by 9 am so that the boat can be cleaned and serviced for the next renter in the afternoon. So if you're moored on the wrong side of the lock between you and the boat hire and those overnight lock closures are in place, you will be late returning the boat and may incur a penalty.[2]

 The clearance under most of the bridges on the canal is exceedingly shallow and sometimes becomes gradually shallower. The person at the tiller will need to be aware that an initial crouch may not be sufficient by the other end of the bridge.

 Unlike most canals, you're advised to leave the chamber drained and the lower gates open after passing through a lock on the Mon & Brec. You should still, however, lower all ground and gate paddles.

## Hiking and cycling challenges

There are very few challenges to cycling or hiking the Monmouthshire & Brecon Canal. The towpath, of course, is very flat and is a mix of surfaces that improves as you approach a village or town. It's a brick or paved path near Brecon Basin, for instance, and crushed stone for much of the length of the canal. The towpath becomes single track

2   There were no lock closures as of August 2019, but climate change will make drought an ever present problem

on the more open stretches of the canal (south of Abergavenny), but in general it is wide and packed. Of course wherever trees cover the towpath you'll find mud after a rain but there are relatively few rutted tracks. The least traveled part of the canal, from Goytre to Pontymoile, is challenging because of vegetation crowding the towpath, but still doable.

 Cyclists should slow for bridges and when passing moored boats. Boaters should clearly mark mooring pins with a handkerchief or grocery bag and not stretch mooring lines across the towpath.

The towpath follows the canal almost continuously except for a short diversion onto the B4558 because of the Ashford Tunnel (375yd/0.21mi/343m). Except for a 2mi/3.2km stretch from Brecon to the Brynich Lock and a 0.6mi/1km section at Govilon, the towpath follows the eastern or northern bank of the canal.

### A bridge too many
The 126 bridges on the canal will wear on you. Many are so low cyclists will need to dismount and many have blind turns. You should ring your bell several times before and while going through a bridge. Fortunately at some bridges the towpath will diverge to go around as well as under.

Gates are another annoyance for cyclists, especially those laden with packs and panniers. You'll see kissing gates, U-shaped gates and cattle gates. Except for the cattle gates, the gates primarily exist to deter motorized vehicles from driving onto the towpath.

*Most CRT restrooms are reasonably pleasant, but the ones at Gilwern are a bit grim*

A good rule to follow in the country is to close any gates you pass through

Off the towpath, you'll find that cycling is more of a challenge. Obviously you'll have more elevation changes, but you'll also have to negotiate the narrow roads that rarely have a shoulder or verge. Hikers, of course, will face the same challenges as cyclists. The market towns of Crickhowell and Abergavenny are about a mile from the canal, which means a long hike, especially if you had bought groceries or souvenirs.

## Bike restrictions

Many of the narrowboat hires prohibit or greatly restrict bringing a bike on board. Ordinarily bikes are stored on the roof of a narrowboat, but the tunnel and low bridges on the canal make that impossible. And given the tight quarters, it's impractical (and messy) to store a bike in the cabin.

An alternative is to bring a folding bike. I rented a **Brompton Bike**  from a dock in Bristol. You can easily store a folding bike in the well deck of most narrowboats—maybe even two if you don't mind giving up seating.

Definitely check the restrictions on any paths at **Sustrans**  and obey any instructions on the trail to dismount. Bikes are generally not allowed on footpaths but are permitted on bridle paths. Horses, however, always have the right of way. If approaching a horse from the opposite direction, cyclists should stop to let the horse pass. If overtaking a horse, ask the rider if you can pass. Take care not to frighten the horses.

## Restrooms/water points

Fortunately there are several CRT facilities, including toilets and showers, scattered along the canal from Brecon to Pontymoile, but on the southern end the toilets are widely spaced and you'll have to rely on pubs for restroom breaks … and there are few pubs. Unfortunately the nature of a canal makes it difficult to pay a call of nature. The towpath is usually pretty exposed and either bordered by vegetation or runs next to a farmer's field.

You'll need a **Waterways key** from the Canal & River Trust if you plan to use these facilities or any of the water points. A Waterways key is provided on hire narrowboats but can be bought from the CRT website even if you're not a boater.

## Camping

Although the canal is almost entirely within the Brecon Beacons National Park, there are, unlike in US national parks or wilderness areas, relatively few places to legally camp. That's because so much of the park is privately owned or common land. There are secluded places to "wild camp," but you'd have to be a local to know them and you run the risk of being run off by park authorities or farmers.

Some farmers, however, make a little income from allowing people to camp and you can find a listing of all the **farm campsites in Wales** at the Duke of Edinburgh's Award website. Click the resources dropdown list to see all options.

## Nettles

When you're trying to relieve yourself *al fresco*, you'll inevitably squat in a bunch of nettles because these stinging plants like water. Aside from washing the affected area the only effective remedies are antihistamines and topical corticosteroids.

## Waterborne disease

Don't swim in the canals and do wash your hands after contact with canal water. Although the risk is low, you run a danger of contracting Weil's disease or leptospirosis transmitted through animal urine.

# Trails

Any cycling or hiking trip along the Monmouthshire & Brecon Canal is aided by the popularity of the Brecon Beacons National Park. Trails criss-cross the park and the canal is part of many of these trails.

### Taff Trail

The **Taff Trail** is a 55mi/88km hiking and biking trail from Brecon to Cardiff Bay and follows the route of National Cycle Route 8.[3] The trail follows the River Taff and takes advantage of the routes of the abandoned Taff Vale Railway and the Glamorganshire Canal.

Taff is a nickname for both people from Cardiff and all of Wales. Some consider it an affectionate nickname, others a derogatory one. It may be a corruption of the common Welsh name Dafydd.

The trail uses the Mon & Brec towpath until Brynich Lock, where it departs the canal to follow the B4558, which parallels the canal for much of its length. The trail, however, leaves the B4558 at Talybont-

---

3    NCR 8 continues north from Brecon all the way to Holyhead on the Isle of Anglesey, an additional 195mi/314km.

*Canoeing, paddleboarding and kayaking are great alternatives to renting a narrowboat*

on-Usk to go south and passes by the Talybont and Pontsticill reservoirs. The trail continues south through Merthyr Tydfil, Abercynon, Pontypridd, Tongwynlais and finally Cardiff.

### NCR 47 and 49

NCR 49 is a 20mi/32.2km cycle path from Newport to Abergavenny and follows the towpath of the Mon & Brec, including the abandoned section of what was the Monmouthshire Canal. It ends where it intersects with NCR 47, a 128mi/206km trail from Newport to Fishguard (on the northern coast of Pembrokeshire). NCR 47 follows the towpath of the Crumlin Arm of the Monmouthshire Canal for 6mi/9.6km and then follows the path of the Sirhowy River.

### Usk Valley Walk

The **Usk Valley Walk** 🚶 is a 48mi/77km walk from Caerleon (near Newport) to Brecon, following the River Usk and then the Mon & Brec. It's a complicated path so you'll need some Ordnance Survey maps to find your way.

 The town of Usk is some distance from the canal (5.1mi/8.2km east of Ponytmoile), but the **Usk Rural Life Museum** 🚶 and its dog, bike and child friendly café is worth a visit while on your valley walk. The museum has more than 5,000 exhibits collected by local enthusiasts to preserve the heritage of the country people in the Welsh Borders.

### Offa's Dyke Path

**Offa's Dyke Path** 🚶 more or less follows the dyke or earthwork created by Offa, the 8th-century King of Mercia, who desired a defensible border with the troublesome Welsh. The 177mi/285km trail runs from Chepstow to Monmouth, skirts Abergavenny and passes through Hay-on-Wye. It continues north, running between the borders of England and Wales (or Powys and Shropshire). The path follows the Llangollen Canal in northern Wales at times before ending at Prestatyn (west of Liverpool). Unfortunately the path is some distance from the Mon & Brec.

*Beacons Water Trail*

The canal and the Usk from Brecon to Talybont-on-Usk are recognized as the Beacons Water Trail. You do need a license to take a canoe on the canal although you're covered if you hire a boat, canoe or other watercraft. Licenses can be obtained through **British Canoeing** 🅦, **Canoe Wales** 🅦 or the **Canal & River Trust** 🅦.

*Cambrian Way*

In 2019 the unofficial 298mi/479km **Cambrian Way** 🅦 from Conwy to Cardiff was officially recognized. After running through the Central Beacons, it approaches the canal from the west, then angles north and crosses the canal at Llangattock/Crickhowell. It loops back, heads south and crosses the canal again at Llanfoist/Abergavenny. The way roughly parallels the canal south to Pontypool/Pontymoile before turning southwest to Cardiff. The way is challenging, following ridge lines and bagging several peaks in the beacons include Pen-y-Fan and Sugar Loaf.

## Boat hires

**Cambrian Cruisers** 🅦, 2.5mi/4km (as measured by the canal) southeast of Brecon Basin, is a family-run business with a fleet of 13 boats, "equally" divided among two-berth, four-berth and six-berth boats. Five of the boats come with an additional toilet.

Jonathan and Camilla Griffiths now run the business after the retirement of Jonathan's parents. Although they have a no bike policy, a folding bike is allowed, but confirm this with an email. Cambrian Cruisers also offers pump out service for £15.

Family-run **Country Craft Narrowboats** 🅦 operates six boats right in the middle of the Llangynidr five-lock flight. It's in one of the prettiest locations on the canal (also next to Canal & River Trust services) and it has the advantage that you can be trained to turn a lock just a hundred feet from where you pick up your boat. Country Craft calls novices their specialty. All the boats are named Country Something and are no more than 50 feet long. The two largest can accommodate four adults

and two children (up to two dogs can travel for free). There's also a twee 37-foot boat that's ideal for a couple.

Country Craft also offers overnight (no cruising) and one-day rentals as a "taster" to see if narrowboating might appeal to you, and pump out service for £15 after 5 pm but not on Sundays or Wednesdays.

 Bow thrusters are impeller- or propeller-driven jets of water that can nudge the front of the boat left or right. They're very useful when casting off, mooring, reversing or

*A narrowboat has all the comforts of home, except a dishwasher. My BFF Lee is washing up in the kitchen.*

making tight turns. Used properly they can help if you've run aground but make sure you don't suck debris into the thrusters. Use thrusters briefly because some electric thrusters can overheat or drain batteries.

**Beacon Park Boats** Ⓦ at Llangattock (about the halfway point of the canal) is another family-run business, offering 19 different luxury boats, most wider than the standard 6-feet 10-inches of a narrowboat (up to 8-feet 6-inches). All of the boats have bow thrusters, several have two toilets and one sports a hot tub. All have Wi-Fi. You will take notice when a Beacon Park Boat passes you with its gleaming brass, potted plants and canopied well deck. Even the complimentary umbrellas supplied with each boat bear the company logo. All of the boats are named after birds.

Beacon Park Boats also offers electric day boat rentals and has three cottages at Llanfoist Wharf to rent. During the winter some of the boats are also used as moored houseboats. Regarding bikes, I am informed: "We generally wouldn't encourage boat hirers to bring their own bikes due to lack of storage space. We do, however, recommend hiring bikes from local companies instead."

**Castle Narrowboats** Ⓦ and **Road House Narrowboats** Ⓦ are both based at Gilwern. For 2020, family-run Castle Narrowboats will offer six diesel-powered narrowboats and two electric-powered boats. Pets are allowed on some boats. The boats run from 45- to 52-feet long with accommodations from two to six. The electric boats sleep four adults and can cruise for up to 18 miles on a charge. Castle has six charging points along the canal—their motto is "Go Green Go Electric"—with moorings reserved for the electric boats. Folding bikes are permitted on boats. The hire offers pump out service for £15.

I'm not sure how I'd feel about cruising on an electric boat. The putt-putt of a diesel boat is actually pretty soothing but I'm sure an electric is a greener option. And, of course, the boats are named after Welsh castles. Castle Narrowboats also rent a VW camper van to explore the countryside.

Yes, Road House Narrowboats is another family-run business and it's the smallest of the boat hires on the canal with just four boats, so book early if you're interested. The longest boat is 42 feet and sleeps four adults. The shortest is 32 feet and sleeps two. I "suspect" the boats are named after welsh slate sizes prefixed by the village name Gilwern. Ask permission to include a folding bike. Pets are allowed. One very nice touch is that the boats are decorated with traditional roses and castle artwork. Road House also offers to pick up travelers from nearby bus or rail stations. Road House does offer pump out service for £15.

Road House Narrowboats also offers a B&B or self-catered room. And most importantly, Road House has a well-stocked gift shop offering locally crafted goods as well as canal and Welsh souvenirs. We stopped here to pick up our Mon & Brec brass plaque and a copy of *200 years of The Monmouthshire and the Brecknock & Abergavenny Canals.*

**Red Line Boats** Ⓦ is located at Goytre Wharf about as far south on the canal as most people want to travel. Red Line is part of the ABC Leisure Group that rents boats across the UK. At Goytre it offers eight boats in two classes, Red Line Finch (at 47-feet long sleeps up to five) and Red Line Swallow (56-feet long, sleeps up to eight and has two toilets). 4G Wi-Fi is offered. First pet is free with an additional charge for a second pet. Red Line also rents a self-catered holiday cottage and day boats (including one with wheelchair access). Sewage pump out is available at £18 and folding bikes that safely fit in the cabin are allowed. Goytre Wharf also offers other attractions such as a summer café, restored lime kilns, slipway, chandlery and a Canal & River Trust Visitor Centre.

All the boat hires listed will give you basic instruction on the operation of the boat, advice on turning locks, mooring, etc. This will take 30 minutes to an hour and there will be an instruction book provided. Your boat will be fueled and it's unlikely it will need to be refueled. It's also unlikely you'll need to pump out the sewage tank.

The boats are supplied with almost everything you need, from linen to cutlery and washing up liquid to wine glasses. You will want to buy groceries but often coffee, tea and milk (and maybe a bottle of wine) are provided for the first day. The boats have every amenity including flush toilets, shower, full kitchen, beds, dining table and seating. For most overseas customers towels are automatically included, but it never hurts to confirm this.

## Bike hire

Full-service **Biped Cycles** 🌐, located on the east side of Usk Bridge in Brecon, will deliver bikes to you. **Hopyard Cycles** 🌐 "will deliver cycles to hotels, guest houses, bed and breakfast establishments and campsites." It's located at Hopyard Farm just north of the canal near Govilon Wharf. It also operates a self-catering holiday cottage that can sleep up to 14 people. **Drover Cycles** 🌐 will deliver bikes within a 20-mile radius of the shop in Hay-on-Wye, which includes much of the canal from Brecon to Abergavenny. **Mountain Tours** 🌐 offers guided hiking and biking trips around Blaenavon and also rents bike for self-guided trips. Pick up points include Govilon Wharf, Goytre Wharf and Pontymoile Basin. **Bikes+Hikes** 🌐 rents bike from a store in Talybont-on-Usk or will deliver a bike "to your hotel, hostel or B&B front door, or even to your tent." Red Line Boats (01873 880516) also offers bike rentals.

## Canoe/kayak/paddleboard rental

**Backwaters** 🌐 is a (yes, you guessed it) family-run business that offers canoe and kayak rentals. You can choose to start at Brecon, Talybont-on-Usk, Gilwern and Pontymoile. Beacon Park Boats and Red Line Boats also offer canoe rentals. Unfortunately I have yet to find a hire company that specifically offers stand up paddleboards.

If you'd like suggestions and recommendations for canoe trips on the Mon & Brec, you can search for that waterway at **canoedaysout.com** 🌐 or at **Paddlepoints** 🌐.

## Luggage transfers

The group tours listed below offer luggage transfers as part of the package, but **Ride & Hike** Ⓦ is a separate transportation and luggage service offered by Taxi Taxi in Brecon. Ride & Hike can also pick up travelers at the airport or train station.

## Group tours

**Celtic Trails Walking Holidays** Ⓦ and **Contours Walking Holidays** Ⓦ offer self-guided walking tours of Wales, although none specifically follow the Mon & Brec. Services include accommodation, luggage transfers and detailed route information. **Exploring Mid Wales** Ⓦ offers a specific self-guided canal walk. **Dragon Trails** Ⓦ offers group hiking and lodging in and around Crickhowell and **Treads and Trails** Ⓦ in Abergavenny offers hiking and biking trips in the Brecon Beacons.

## Maps

Once on the towpath or on the water it's almost impossible to get lost on the canal, but unless you have GPS it's not always easy to know exactly where you are or what's nearby. Fortunately many maps are available.

### Paid maps/guides

**Ordnance Survey** Ⓦ maps are the gold standard for topographical maps, but frankly they're far too detailed for boating. They are invaluable, however, if you're hiking and following old tramroads and footpaths. OS Landranger maps 160 and 161 cover most of the national park. The addition of Landranger 171 would cover the entire length of the canal. Unfortunately three paper maps would be cumbersome, but paper map purchases also include a free downloadable mobile map. Hikers trying to follow the Usk Valley Walk might want to buy the more detailed OS Explorer maps.

The best boating guide to the canal is **The Mon and Brec Guide** Ⓦ, currently edited by Phil Hughes. The guide goes back to 1991 and its original author, John Norris. Your boat hire may include a copy of this guide.[4] The guide offers an amazingly detailed tour of the canal and every time you exclaim "What's that?" as you pass something on the canal, you can be sure it will be explained in its pages.

The Pearson's **Welsh Waters Canal Companion** Ⓦ is also an excellent guide, but less detailed as it also includes the Shropshire Union, Llangollen and Montgomery canals in addition to the Mon & Brec. The **Collins**

---

4    Our boat hire, Cambrian Cruisers, sent us a copy when we booked our boat

**Nicholson Waterways Guides—Four Counties & The Welsh Canals** —is another excellent guide and is based on OS maps, but in a convenient spiral-bound format.

You can also buy a downloadable map of the canal from **Waterway Routes**  and even better the website offers a free download of the Crumlin Arm and the under restoration section of the Monmouthshire Canal.

### Free maps/guides

The online maps created by the **Canal & River Trust**  are the most up-to-date maps, showing services and navigation and closure notices. **Open Canal Map**  is also excellent for showing canal specific detail and has the advantage of being an app for smartphones.

**CanalPlanAC**  is an online canal planning resource and guide for narrowboaters. You can query any spot on the canals and see what moorings and services are available, and you can plan a trip almost down to the minute. You can select a canal, pick a start and end point, specify how many hours cruising you want to do and have CanalPlanAC suggest moorings for each night of the journey.

Google Maps, of course, is also an excellent resource and can be accessed on your home computer or smartphone. Google maps can also be downloaded in tablet or smartphone apps for offline use. There's even a short-section of the canal at Brecon that you can virtually walk in **StreetView** .

**OpenStreetMap**  won't show traffic congestion or find cheap prices on hotel rooms, but it will show you a lot of user-contributed data such as trails and paths that won't even be found at the Ordnance Survey online.

 Canal &
River Trust
bit.ly/2UjXo4t

 Monmouthshire,
Brecon &
Abergavenny Canals
Trust
bit.ly/2FDxmB2

 National Rail
Journey Planner
bit.ly/2Q3pGdN

 Traveline
Cymru
bit.ly/2yH2rjb

 Open
Signal
bit.ly/2FLD0k2

 Highway
Code
bit.ly/2Q2nAed

 Roundabout
video
bit.ly/2KzRKGG

 CRT boater's
guide
bit.ly/2SrVw5z

 CRT navigation
notices
bit.ly/2z8tTWC

Sustrans
bit.ly/2BBimAV

 Waterways
key
bit.ly/2ZhdLNL

 Duke of Edinburgh's
Award campsite list
bit.ly/30sDtQy

 Taff
Trail
bit.ly/2MBla7H

 Usk Valley
Walk
bit.ly/2IcLapl

 Usk Rural
Life Museum
bit.ly/31pHDsC

 Offa's Dyke
Path
bit.ly/2DDK4gT

 Cambrian Way
bit.ly/2YQHZd0

 British
Canoeing
bit.ly/2FuFaUS

 Canoe
Wales
bit.ly/2XuNH4A

 CRT
canoe license
bit.ly/310IQuk

 canoedaysout.com
bit.ly/2KAnaN3

 paddlepoints
bit.ly/2X4LPzY

## Boat hires

 Cambrian
Cruisers
bit.ly/2yDj5Ao

 Country Craft
Narrowboats
bit.ly/2JokQ8v

 Beacon Park
Boats
bit.ly/2Q2qWOl

 Castle
Narrowboats
bit.ly/2AyMP2M

 Road House
Narrowboats
bit.ly/2yElsTv

 Red Line
Boats
bit.ly/2EOlcGU

## Bike hires

 Brompton
Bike Hire
bit.ly/2Jly06c

 Biped
Cycles
bit.ly/2RmpTsP

 Hopyard
Cycles
bit.ly/2ENlSMU

 Drover
Cycles
bit.ly/2AxTMRm

 Mountain
Tours
bit.ly/2OZ1cGc

 Bikes
+Hikes
bit.ly/2yFaoFD

## Canoe rentals

 Backwaters
bit.ly/2PsN7jV

## Luggage transfer

 Ride
& Hike
bit.ly/2qlCeCn

## Group tours

 Celtic Trails
Walking Holidays
bit.ly/2S3AXeq

 Contours Walking
Holidays
bit.ly/2SwTfKh

 Exploring
Mid Wales
bit.ly/2S3uRuo

 Treads
and Trails
bit.ly/2Kx5odC

 Dragon
Trails
bit.ly/2MRApcM

## Maps/Guides

Ordnance
Survey
bit.ly/2TLXZIh

The Mon and Brec
Guide
bit.ly/2BDhkEH

Welsh Waters
Canal Companion
bit.ly/2tl6gYh

Collins Nicholson
Waterways Guides
bit.ly/2UZamku

Waterway
Routes
bit.ly/31NNLvv

Canal & River
Trust maps
bit.ly/2S3offL

Open
Canal Map
bit.ly/2SzbGxH

CanalPlanAC
bit.ly/2SwhUhU

Mon & Brec
Street View
bit.ly/2tpRmji

OpenStreetMap
bit.ly/2LXy9QA

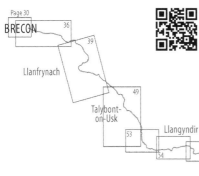

# Canal map key

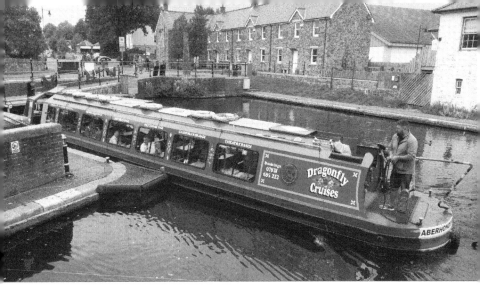

*A Dragonfly Cruises boat returns to Brecon Basin*

# Brecon to Talybont-on-Usk
(6.9mi/11.1km)[1]

Sitting just within the park's northern boundary, the market town of Brecon is a perfect portal to the Brecon Beacons National Park. You can't start a narrowboat trip in Brecon—there's no boat hire—but it's the natural beginning of a cycling or walking holiday on the canal.

Even though it's not the most picturesque town on the canal, it's a pleasant place to walk and the people are very friendly and extremely helpful. Of course this could be said of almost everyone you'll meet in Wales.

## Brecon

The town is primarily a collection of Georgian and Victorian buildings, although there are ancient buildings in Brecon, including the cathedral and the remains of a castle. Most of the houses are stone, brick or whitewashed but you will find a hint of the pastel hues common to waterside towns. The population is more than 8,000, but that climbs considerably in the summer months with park tourists. If you come in August or October, there are many festivals to enjoy that could affect your trip, so plan accordingly.

The town is surrounded by hills and sits in the valley created by the River Usk, which flows through Brecon and is the water source for the

---

1   From Brecon Basin to Bridge No. 144 (Talybont lift bridge)

BRECON

BRECON CANAL BASIN

Mon & Brec Canal

To Talybont »

Bridge, aqueduct and lock numbers are shown in gray

## ⊞ Chemist
1 Boots
2 Well Brecon

## Miscellaneous
1 Brecon Car Rentals
  Bus interchange
  Bike rental
  Theatre Brecheiniog
  Coliseum Cinema
  Fun boat rental
? Brecon Visitor Information
  Parking

## Canal features
  Charging point
  Elsan disposal
  Lock
  Mooring
  Pump out
  Restrooms
  Rubbish
  Showers
  Towpath
  Waterpoint
  Winding hole

## 🍴 Fish and Chips
1 Brecon Fish Bar
2 Watergate Fish Bar & Cafe
3 West End Fish Bar

## ☕ Cafés
1 Café, The
2 Casa Cafe
3 Cat Soup Kitchen
4 Coffee #1 Brecon
5 Coffee Box
6 Costa Coffee
7 Dutchess Café Bistro
8 Greggs
9 St. Mary's Bakery

## 📖 Bookstores
1 Brecon Books
2 Hours Cafe, The
3 WH Smith

## 🛍 Shopping
1 Brecon Convenience Store
2 Brecon Market Hall
3 Cotswold Outdoors
4 Gibb Outdoors
5 Mountain Warehouse
6 Nicholls Brecon

## Accommodations
5 Coach House, The
6 Flag and Castle House
7 Grange Guest House, The
8 Kingfisher's Reach
9 Old Castle Farm
10 Swan Bank Cottage
11 Ty Helg Guest House

## 🍽 Pubs/restaurants
1 Bank Bar & Kitchen
2 Brecon Tap
3 Chang Tai Cuisine
4 Drovers Arms
5 Gurkha Corner, The
6 Pilgrim's Tearoom & Restaurant
7 Rorke's Drift, The
8 Sara Siddons Inn
9 Three Horseshoes Inn, The

## 🍔 Fast food/takeaway
1 Brecon Chicken & Pizza Land
2 Brecon Kebab House
3 La Belle Pizza
4 Little Italy
5 Llanfaes Dairy Ice Cream Bar
6 Proper Pizza, The
7 Subway

## 🏛 Museums
1 Brecknock Museum & Art Gallery
2 Regimental Museum of the Royal Welsh

## 🛒 Groceries
1 Aldi
2 Co-op
3 Morrison's

## ⛪ Churches
1 Brecon Cathedral
2 St. Mary's Church Brecon
3 St. Michael's Catholic Church

## 🏨 Hotels
1 Castle of Brecon Hotel
2 Clarence Inn
3 George Hotel
4 Markets Tavern Hotel Brecon
5 Wellington Hotel

## 🛏 Bed & Breakfast
1 Beacons Guesthouse
2 Borderers Guest House
3 Bridge Cafe Bed & Breakfast
4 Canal Bridge Holiday

canal. There are a number of outdoor outfitters in town if you forgot to bring a fleece or hiking boots for your trek across the Beacons. In fact being a market town there's plenty of shopping and it's a good place to stock up on supplies at the three grocery stores. There's even a cinema if you get bored.

The narrow streets can make traffic challenging and any construction can confound a driver. The main road into town from the east is Watton or the B4601. From the east it's the A40 and A470, but fortunately those roads are routed around the town.

Many of the self-catered cottages and bed and breakfasts can be found on Watton, but there are also two large hotels near the town center and several inns with accommodations. For those who prefer to rough it, there are two caravan and camping sites nearby.

## Attractions

**The Promenade** 🅦 is a 2,600ft/792m path that follows the river just north of the Usk Bridge. It's an easy and surprisingly pastoral walk because there are few buildings on the west (or south) bank of the river. It's anchored by the Promenade Car Park off Fenni-Fach Road and the Watergate Car Park just south of the Brecon Castle Hotel. You can enjoy great views of the Usk Bridge and your path will take you next to the weir that diverts water to the canal. The walk is wheelchair accessible.

The eastern end of the Promenade is next to Watergate Bridge, under which the Honddu meets the Usk. (The Welsh name for the town is Aberhonddu.) There's a boathouse at the western end of the walk where you can rent a rowboat or pedalo (pedal/paddle-powered boat). There's also a café, arcade and the world's smallest go-kart track.

**Brecon Cathedral** 🅦 was the

Wales has a long history of military service, from the Welsh bowmen who fought at Agincourt, to the various regiments of what is now the Royal Welsh who fought during the American Revolutionary War; the Napoleonic Wars; Crimean War; Anglo-Zulu and Anglo-Boer wars; the world wars; and today in Iraq and Afghanistan.

You may also notice Nepalese Gurkha soldiers staying at hotels in Brecon.

*Sphinx cap badge of the South Wales Borderers*

They're part of the Gurkha Wing (Mandalay) and may be instructors or students at the Infantry Battle School in Brecon. About 90 Nepalese families now call Brecon home.

*Brecon Market Hall*

Benedictine Priory of St John the Evangelist founded in 1093. After Henry VIII's dissolution of the monasteries in 1537 it became Brecon Parish Church. It was only named a cathedral in 1927. The cathedral has plaques and stained glass that honor the men of Brecon who fought as bowmen for Henry V at Agincourt. The Havard Chapel in the cathedral also honors the soldiers of the South Wales Borderers (24th Regiment of Foot), who are best known for the battles of Isandlwana and Rorke's Drift in modern-day South Africa.

There's a very nice Pilgrims Tea Rooms & Restaurant situated in the cathedral's old tithe barn. It's open from 9 am–5 pm Mon–Sat and 9 am–4 pm Sunday.

The **Brecon Farmers Market** ⓦ is open from 9:30 am to 2 pm the second Saturday of every month.

An outdoor market is held on the fourth Saturday of the month from April to November between 10 am and 1 pm.

The **Brecknock Museum & Art Gallery** ⓦ, in what was the Victorian-era Shire Hall, is being renovated as part of a £9 million Heritage Lottery Fund grant. The money will also create a new library, community spaces and café. The museum and art gallery collection includes local archaeological artifacts; agricultural tools; natural history and geological specimens; and historic and modern art. The museum will also feature a reconstruction of the Assize Court. The new Y Gaer Cultural Hub was supposed to be opened by late 2018, but rising costs and mating puffins have delayed the reopening.

**Theatr Brycheiniog** ⓦ is a performance space right at the terminus of the Monmouthshire & Brecon Canal. You could hear a jazz band; watch a Shakespearean play or ballet; or view artwork documenting the history of the canal at the theater. Of course there's also a café and occasional outdoor performances by local musicians.

The **Regimental Museum of The Royal Welsh** ⓦ, formerly the South Wales Borderers Museum, is next to the rather forbidding barracks that serve as the headquarters of the 160th (Wales) Infantry Brigade. Although the barracks were sold in 2017, the Ministry of Defence has said the military will continue to have a presence in Brecon. Opening times for the museum are complicated, but it's generally open from 10 am–5 pm Mon–Fri.

If you like lime kilns *(see page 64)*, you can embark on a little off towpath excursion to see the **Watton kilns** just south

*The Castle of Brecon Hotel. Credit: cowbridgeguide.co.uk Wikimedia CC BY 3.0* bit.ly/2KjyGtW

of the towpath. The unnamed road that runs beside the towpath from Brecon Basin departs the canal just east of Bridge 165. Travel east for about 600 feet and look to the north to see the kilns buried underneath a grove of trees.

If you haven't done enough walking or cycling, you could also visit Pen y Crug Hill Fort (1,086ft/331m) and along the way stop at Maendu Well, a "holy spring" that probably supplied water to Brecon Castle. Some ramparts of the hill fort remain and the stepped structure of the defenses are still obvious. From the canal basin, this would be a 4.3mi/6.9km round trip. See my **online map** 🅦 for details.

## Festivals

The **Brecon County Show** 🅦 is held the first Saturday of August at The Showground south of the canal. There are cattle, sheep, horse, pony and goat classes and poultry shows

as well as a shearing competition. Exhibitors offer local produce, farm machinery, clothing and jewelry. There's also a dog show, food hall and fun fair.

**Brecon Fringe Festival** 🅦 runs for four days in August. Venues, which are scattered all over town, book performers, musical and otherwise, and most events are free. Venues include outdoor stages featuring full bands, solo guitarists on street corners, pubs, restaurants and even the cathedral.

Concurrent with the Fringe Festival is the **Brecon Jazz Festival** 🅦 , which over the years has attracted a number of well known artists, including Joan Armatrading, Amy Winehouse, Allen Toussaint, Jools Holland and Mavis Staples. Most of the jazz events charge admission.

Also in August is **Volksfest Wales** 🅦 at The Showground south of the canal, where you can ogle every manifestation of vehicle produced by Volkswagen.

## Llangorse Lake

If you're a cyclist and don't mind riding on narrow one-lane roads, there's a 4.6mi/7.4km trip from Brynich Lock to **Llangorse Lake**  that's very rewarding. The unnamed road from the lock is mostly two lanes with a little grassy shoulder, but

*Crannog visitor center on Llangorse Lake*
*Credit: pxhere* bit.ly/2yzVu32

sometimes drops to one lane. It's a fairly straight, well-maintained and not busy road, but you might have to flatten yourself against bushes at times. The speed limit is 60 mph, based on the national speed limit for a single carriageway. There's an alternative route to the lake from Talybont-on-Usk described and you can see both routes at **my online map** .

Llangorse Lake—the largest natural lake in Wales—has a lot to offer, including fishing and water sports, with dinghy, windsurfing, canoe, kayaking, stand-up paddleboard, pedalo and rowboat rentals. There are several churches, caravan and camping parks, pubs, self-catered cottages and B&Bs and even a horse-riding center.

Another attraction is the only (known) crannog in Wales and England. More common in Scotland and Ireland, crannogs are artificial islands created on lakes usually connected to the shore by easily defended causeways. The Llangorse crannog was a royal "house" of the King of Brycheiniog and was attacked and destroyed in 916 CE by the forces of Æthelflæd, Lady of the Mercians (and daughter of Alfred the Great).

The crannog is about 170 feet in diameter and is about 125 feet from shore. The interpretive center for the crannog is housed in a recreation of one of the conical huts that might have stood on the island. The royal house, however, was probably a little grander and wooden palisades would have protected the island.

The lake's history also has to compete with myth and legend. There are stories of the lake, after an earthquake, swallowing a palace and even the Roman city of Loventium. Further, the lake is said to be the home of Gorsey, an afanc or lake monster. As the lake is not very deep, that's unlikely, however some monstrous pike have been caught there. Water voles and otters do call the lake home.

In October you'll find the **Brecon Baroque Festival** ⑩, featuring groups like the Society of Strange and Ancient Instruments and the Brecon Baroque Festival Orchestra. All the events are paid, indoors (except for a guided walk in the Brecon Beacons) and most are at Theatr Brycheiniog. And of course there's also a concurrent Brecon Baroque Fringe, because why not?

Also in October is the **Brecon Beacons Food Festival** ⑩ with exhibitors at the Brecon Indoor Market.

The final item on this list isn't quite a festival, but is festive. **The Canalathon** ⑩, originally sponsored by the Momounthshire, Brecon & Abergavenny Canal Trust and the Canal & River Trust, ends at Brecon Basin, having started in Pontymoile Basin earlier in the day. Four-person teams canoe, bike and walk (or run) the 35-mile length of the canal. Although it's meant to be an annual event, it skipped 2018, but did take place in 2019.

## Hotels

The **Wellington Hotel** ⑩ is a fine old Georgian building overlooking the statue of the Duke of Wellington. It's essentially on the High Street and is about a 0.25mi/0.4km

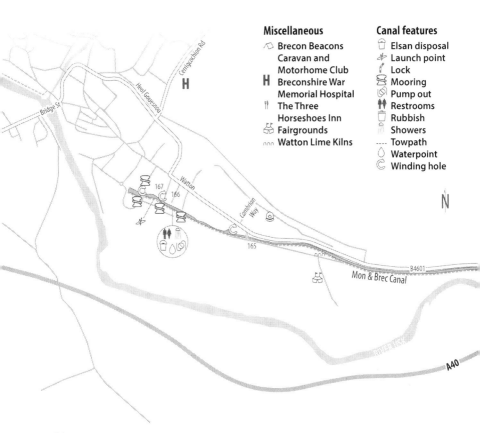

**Miscellaneous**
- Brecon Beacons Caravan and Motorhome Club
- **H** Breconshire War Memorial Hospital
- The Three Horseshoes Inn
- Fairgrounds
- Watton Lime Kilns

**Canal features**
- Elsan disposal
- Launch point
- Lock
- Mooring
- Pump out
- Restrooms
- Rubbish
- Showers
- Towpath
- Waterpoint
- Winding hole

walk to the canal terminus basin. The 24-room hotel is owned by SA Brains Brewery. There are several wheelchair accessible rooms and a hot breakfast is included. The hotel offers secure bike storage but no parking. There are, however, nearby pay-and-display car parks with free overnight parking. It is listed as dog friendly.

**The George Hotel** 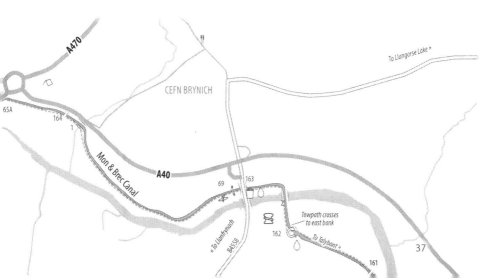 is a four-room hotel in a 16th-century coaching inn at the upper end of the High Street (less than a 0.5mi/0.8km walk to the canal basin). It's a JD Wetherspoon property. Like the Wellington, there's no parking, but car parks are nearby. Secure bike storage is available.

The rather grand 38-room **Castle of Brecon Hotel** incorporates a wall and tower from an 11th-century Norman castle. It has a view looking down onto the river and bridge and has limited on-site parking. The hotel offers disabled access rooms and also cottages, self-catered and family rooms. The hotel is very convenient to the Promenade and is a 0.5mi/0.8km walk to the canal basin.

The 5-room **Markets Tavern** (near what was the Brecon livestock market) is just over a 0.25mi/0.4km walk to the canal basin. Two of the rooms share a bathroom but the rest are en suite. A free breakfast as well as secure bike storage are included. All the rooms are above the pub/restaurant. The rooms are not disabled accessible. Pets are welcome.

At a tenth of a mile (0.16km), **The Clarence Inn** with four rooms, is the closest hotel to the canal. It's a former coaching inn and offers a free full breakfast.

## Bed and breakfast/self-catering

There are too many B&Bs in Brecon to list them all so I'll just include the ones most convenient to the canal. (Most of the B&Bs are found along Watton and along the B4601.)
- **Ty Helyg Guest House**
- **The Grange Guest House**

*Cambrian Cruisers at Llanfrynach with a view toward the Central Beacons*
*Credit: James Bates*

- **Borderers Guesthouse**
- **Canal Bridge Holiday Accommodation**
- **Swan Bank Cottage**

## Camping
**Bishops Meadow Caravan & Camping Park**  is about 1.5mi/2.4km from the canal basin in Brecon and offers toilets and showers, laundry facilities and even has an on-site restaurant.

**Cefn Cantref Campsite**  is about 2.1mi/3.4km from the canal basin. Facilities include toilets and showers and a tuck shop (small café/food store). These camp sites are not shown on the maps in this book, however you will find **Brecon Beacons Caravan Club Site** at Brynich on the previous page. Although it's a membership scheme, non-members

can book.

## Pubs/restaurants/fast food
I can't list all the pubs, restaurants and coffee shops, so this is just a list of places that appeal to me or that I've visited. Of course the hotels previously listed have pubs or restaurants and I've enjoyed meals at the Wellington and George hotels.

**The Gurkha Corner**  offers Nepalese food. Next time I'll order the nettle curry to take my revenge for all the times I've been stung.

**The Bank Bar & Kitchen**  (formerly The Puzzle Tree) is a gastropub just opposite the Brecknock Museum. Brecon is wonderfully free of fast-food chain restaurants, but there are a number of quick and cheap food options, including:
- **Brecon Fish Bar**

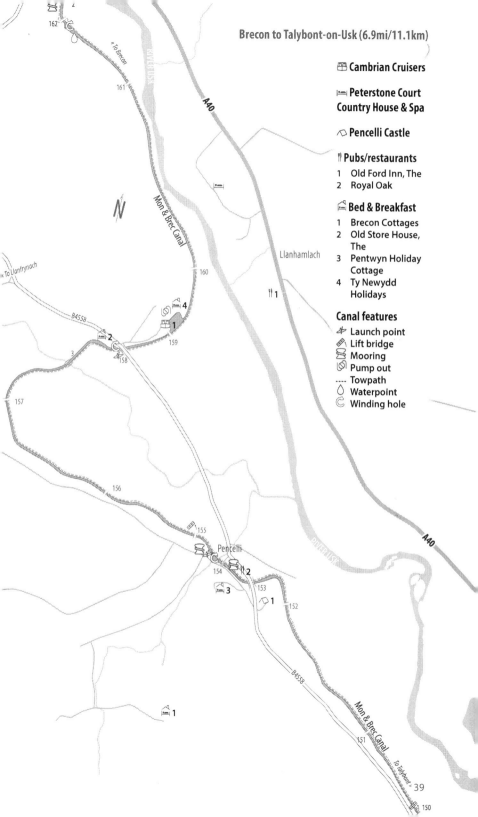

# Brecon to Talybont-on-Usk (6.9mi/11.1km)

🛏 **Cambrian Cruisers**

🛏 **Peterstone Court
Country House & Spa**

🏰 **Pencelli Castle**

🍴 **Pubs/restaurants**
1 Old Ford Inn, The
2 Royal Oak

🛏 **Bed & Breakfast**
1 Brecon Cottages
2 Old Store House,
  The
3 Pentwyn Holiday
  Cottage
4 Ty Newydd
  Holidays

**Canal features**
⚓ Launch point
🌉 Lift bridge
🪢 Mooring
💧 Pump out
---- Towpath
💧 Waterpoint
🌀 Winding hole

Llanhamlach

To Llanfrynach

Mon & Brec Canal

To Brecon

A40

Pencelli

B4558

To Talybont

- **Brecon Kebab House**
- **Brecon Chicken and Pizza Land**

## Services

**Biped Cycles**  is a full-service bike shop that rents bikes by the day or week and will deliver bikes to you.

## Transportation

There's no train service to Brecon but there are a number of bus stops, a **car hire**  and several **taxi services** .

## Llanfrynach

From Brecon the canal travels southwest, crossing the Usk at Cefn Brynich, which is a community of the village of Llanfrynach. The canal actually passes between the villages of Llanfrynach and Llanhamlach. Before the aqueduct over the Usk,

*Near Pencelli, the first of six lift bridges (number 155) on the canal*

however, you'll encounter Brynich Lock, the first lock after leaving Brecon. It's actually numbered Lock 69. Because of drought conditions it may be locked between 6 pm and 10 am. It's a great first lock for beginners because the other locks on the canal are part of a flight, which requires a little more awareness of traffic. It's also the least likely to have a volunteer lockkeeper in attendance, so you have a chance to turn a lock unsupervised. Brynich Lock is unusual because it's the only lock on the canal with hydraulic winding gears (easier to turn) on the lower gate paddles.

The Brynich Aqueduct over the Usk was designed and built by Thomas Dadford Junior. Dadford was the engineer for the Brecknock & Abergavenny and the Monmouthshire canals, and worked for his father on the Stourbridge, Glamorganshire and Neath canals. The last (or first) bridge on the Mon & Brec at Brecon Basin is named Dadfords Bridge. Dadford died aged just 40 in 1801.

If you're returning a narrowboat to Cambrian Cruisers in the morning, the mooring just south of the Usk Aqueduct is a perfect place to spend the last night of your trip. There's even a water point on the east (or north) bank of the canal. Incidentally there's a winding hole here used by the Dragonfly tour boat to turn around for the trip back to Brecon.

The aqueduct is a little unusual in having a walkable path on either side but the towpath is on the west side. It's possible to walk down to the river from the east side of the aqueduct. When the water flow is low, you can even walk to the middle of the river on curiously rectangular rock slabs (please use caution if you attempt this).

Immediately after the aqueduct at Bridge 162, the canal towpath switches from the west (or south) bank to the east bank, where it remains for most of the canal. If you're cycling or walking north, you might be tempted to go under the bridge but unless you want to walk down to the river, you should cross the bridge.

Llanhamlach, on the other side of the Usk from the canal, is little more than a church, hotel and pub. Unfortunately it's difficult from the canal to get to either **Peterstone Country House & Spa**  (a hotel) or the **Old Ford Inn**  (a pub with rooms). After the Brynich Aqueduct, the canal runs south of the Usk and the only nearby bridge over the river is where the B4558 crosses the A40. To get to either requires traveling a mile or more on the A40, doable but not pleasant as there is no sidewalk, however one could walk or ride on the grass verge.

 As you leave Brecon, there are great views towards the Central Beacons thanks to breaks in the trees on the west or south bank of the canal. The best views are as the canal approaches Llanfrynach.

It's difficult to get to Llanfrynach either by bike or on foot because the B4558 is barely a two-lane road with no shoulder and closely bordered by vegetation, but you only have to travel 0.36mi/0.58km before the turn off. The village is pleasant enough but with no pubs (The White Swan Inn is permanently closed), stores or other attractions, not very rewarding. The **Ty Mawr Luxury Cottage Collection** , however, looks very attractive for those not on a budget.

 You're really missing out if you spend all the time on your boat. Get out and walk the towpath and stand on bridges to get enough elevation to see over the vegetation that obscures the view.

Cambrian Cruisers *(see page 27)* is the most northerly narrow-boat hire on the canal and you'll also find the associated **Ty Newydd**

*St. Mary's Church in Brecon with a statue of the Duke of Wellington in front. The Wellington Hotel is to the left.*

**Holidays** Ⓦ here with self-catered cottages and B&B rooms. Just down the canal from Cambrian Cruisers you'll find a very distinctive B&B at **The Old Storehouse** Ⓦ. It's more like being the house guest of a mildly eccentric host, but the rooms look lovely and the conservatory is charming.

After leaving Cambrian Cruisers and just before arriving at Pencelli you'll encounter your first lift bridge (one of five) at a farm. If on a narrowboat, you'll need a windlass to turn the hydraulic winding gear (tedious but not too strenuous) that lifts the bridge, and you should lower it after leaving. It offers no impediment to cyclists or hikers except the need to open and close the livestock gates.

**Forge Cottage** Ⓦ is a rather luxe self-catered cottage between Pencelli and Talybont-on-Usk. It has three bedrooms and the nice amenity of a washing machine. It has an unbelievably beautiful location.

## Pencelli

Continuing down the canal you'll come to the village of Pencelli, which apart from a few homes consists of the family-run **Royal Oak** Ⓦ, **Pencelli Castle** Ⓦ caravan camp and **Pentwyn Holiday Cottage** Ⓦ. The cottage is a restored barn with two bedrooms and can sleep four people.

The Royal Oak is a great pub and wonderfully convenient to the canal thanks to several moorings. We were told at Cambrian Cruisers that it's possible to order at the pub and take food to your boat.

Pencelli Castle (very little remains of the 11<sup>th</sup>-century Norman castle) is a family-run caravan and camping park. Cyclists and hikers can pitch a tent and use the toilets, showers and laundry facilities. There's an on-site shop that offers local produce.

## Information & maps

 Visit
Brecon
bit.ly/2WoXCV8

 Brecon
walk/cycle map
bit.ly/2TX9hxO

 Llangorse Lake
walk/cycle map
bit.ly/2YotbAp

## Attractions

 Brecon
Promenade
bit.ly/2Am2P7S

 Brecon
Cathedral
bit.ly/2PkDX9a

 Brecon Farmers
Market
bit.ly/2OHTtMH

 Brecknock Museum
& Art Gallery
bit.ly/2CYI5Wh

 Theatr
Brycheiniog
bit.ly/2OFchMH

 Reg'l Museum
of The Royal Welsh
bit.ly/2R5vyDK

 Watton
lime kilns
bit.ly/2Cyd9v4

 Llangorse
Lake
bit.ly/2O5GxuJ

## Festivals

 Brecon
County Show
bit.ly/2OD9pQa

 Brecon
Fringe Festival
bit.ly/2ODcjEy

 Brecon
Jazz Festival
bit.ly/2CxRZx9

 Volksfest
Wales
bit.ly/2yRflue

 Brecon
Baroque Festival
bit.ly/2EECbLQ

 Brecon Beacons
Food Festival
bit.ly/2q5rCHq

 Canalathon
bit.ly/2XvJRJs

## Lodging

*Hotels*

 Wellington
Hotel
bit.ly/2S7Knqx

 The George
Hotel
bit.ly/2Anazqh

 The Castle of
Brecon Hotel
bit.ly/2NXutfe

 The Markets
Tavern
bit.ly/2Jbm0nJ

 The Clarence Inn
bit.ly/2PkTu8Y

 Peterstone Country
House & Spa
bit.ly/2OQNchz

 The Old
Ford Inn
bit.ly/2CGJn7v

*B&Bs/self-catering*

 Ty Helyg
Guest House
bit.ly/2yWeRTB

 The Grange
Guest House
bit.ly/2R50QKI

# The Monmouthshire & Brecon Canal

 Borderers
Guesthouse
bit.ly/2S7dhHv

 Cefn Cantref
Campsite
bit.ly/2NXwhow

 ALDI
bit.ly/2ELYbUW

 Canal Bridge Holiday
Accommodation
bit.ly/2OFsFwp

 Brecon Beacons
Caravan Club Site
bit.ly/2YodcSg

 Co-op
bit.ly/2CK2MEP

 Swan Bank
Cottage
bit.ly/2Sbjqm2

 Pencelli
Castle
bit.ly/2CI1WrZ

 Brecon Convenience
goo.gl/maps/
nLsJvvMvjgB2

*Llanfrynach*

## Pubs/restaurants

*Bookstores*

 Ty Newydd
Holidays
bit.ly/2OOmt5o

 Gurkha
Corner
bit.ly/2S9Hwxh

 WH
Smith
bit.ly/2KXpyhc

 Ty Mawr Luxury
Cottage Collection
bit.ly/2RFvD2u

 Bank Bar &
Kitchen
bit.ly/2PKIGhb

 Brecon Books
goo.gl/maps/
Mnfq7HQYP9p

 The Old
Storehouse
bit.ly/2JhPxwd

 Brecon
Fish Bar
bit.ly/2qbiqS1

 The
Hours
bit.ly/2YAeEkC

*Pencelli*

 Forge
Cottage
bit.ly/2JhDuih

 Brecon
Kebab House
bit.ly/2O3lJnU

 The
Works
bit.ly/2RgF8DK

*Pharamcy*

 Pentwyn
Cottage
bit.ly/2SmxxoE

 Brecon Chicken and
Pizza Land
bit.ly/2Re1llW

 Boots
bit.ly/2KXTQQW

*Pencelli*

 Brecon
Cottages
bit.ly/2Yp8wvy

 The Royal Oak
bit.ly/2PYupO2

 Well
Brecon
bit.ly/2xpDkQX

## Camping

## Shopping

*Outfitters*

*Grocery*

 Bishops Meadow
Caravan & Camping
bit.ly/2PNGh5j

  Morrisons
bit.ly/2JgNPuS

 Cotswolds
Outdoors
bit.ly/2RhtqbX

*What a difference a little blue sky can make. The sign post indicates the towpath near Brecon is part of the Taff Trail. Credit: James Bates*

 Mountain Warehouse
bit.ly/2qfP0qx

## Services

 Biped Cycles
bit.ly/2ApiCTr

 Visit Brecon
bit.ly/2z7nH0T

 Breconshire War Memorial Hospital
bit.ly/2Rhvb93

## Transportation

 Brecon Car Rentals
bit.ly/2Lc0Clu

 Johns Taxi (TAXI TAXI)
bit.ly/2J4EuXt

Ask4Taxi
7779 862223

Brecon Taxis
1874 623444

Neils Taxi
7970 448385

## Boat hire

 Dragonfly Cruises
bit.ly/2kqsN5j

*There are many pubs to choose from on the Mon & Brec, especially between Pencelli and Abergavenny. This is the White Hart Inn in Talybont-on-Usk, one of three choices just along the side of the canal.*

*Several of the bridges on the canal are quite low, as you can see by my husband ducking under Bridge 128*

*Every once in a while the canal offers a stunning view of the surrounding hills, like here at Bridge 126 east of Llangynidr*

# Talybont-on-Usk to Crickhowell
(8.1mi/13.1km)[1]

## Talybont-on-Usk

Talybont-on-Usk (not to be confused with Tal-y-bont village just north of Aberystwyth, also in Wales) is the first substantial village you encounter after leaving Brecon. I've always imagined the inhabitants of Talybont-on-Usk to be strapping athletes based on the number of recreational activities in the area. There's a special emphasis on biking, but there are also a number of hiking trails ranging from a relaxing poetry walk to the long distance Taff Trail. The village boasts several pubs and rental cottages, campgrounds and even a café/store. More information can be found at the **village website** ⓦ.

Between Pencelli and Talybont-on-Usk you'll encounter three lift bridges. Leave them in the position you found them. Bridge 148 is almost always raised.

---

1   To Ffawyddog Bridge, No. 116

The views from the canal really don't do the surrounding hills justice. Talybont is a perfect place to rent a bike and ride up the 1,808ft/551m Tor y Foel, which is a hill on the eastern flank of Talybont reservoir and forest. From the summit you can see half of the national park.

## Festivals

The **Talybont Show** Ⓦ is held every year on the August Bank Holiday Saturday with livestock and dog shows, horse judging and crafts and food marquees.

The two-day **Over the Baas** Ⓦ mountain bike festival is held in and around Talybont in September. It's a ticketed event if you want to participate in the big rides (25–30 miles) but there are free events.

## Pubs/Hotels

Although there are no hotels as such in Talybont, you can book rooms at **The White Hart, The Travellers Restaurant and Rooms, The Star Inn** and **The Usk Inn** Ⓦ. The first three inns can be found along on the canal with The Usk Inn just a quarter mile north on Station Road.

The White Hart is a 300-year-old coaching inn and has four bunk-house rooms accommodating 20 guests with a communal breakfast kitchen. The Star Inn has two rooms with optional breakfast provided at Talybont Stores. The Travellers Rest has two rooms and a studio apartment, all with provided breakfast. The Usk Inn has 10 bedrooms with full breakfast.

## Bed and breakfast/self-catering
• **Aber Farm shepherd's hut** Ⓦ
• **Arches at Bailey Barn** Ⓦ
• **Belvedere Bed & Breakfast** Ⓦ
• **Cui Hen Beudy Cottage** Ⓦ
• **Coity Bach Self Catering Holiday** Ⓦ
• **Forge Cottage** Ⓦ
• **Gilestone Farm** Ⓦ
• **Hawthorns, The** Ⓦ
• **School Annex** Ⓦ

### 🛒 Groceries
1 Talybont Stores Cafe & Post Office

### ⛪ Churches
1 St. Ffraid
2 Talachddu Church

### 🍺 Pubs/Hotels
1 Star Inn, The
2 Travellers Rest, The
3 Usk In, The
4 White Hart, The

### 🏠 Bed & Breakfast
1 Aber Farm shepherd's hut
2 Arches at Baileys Barn
3 Belvedere Bed & Breakfast
4 Cui Hen Beudy Cottage
5 Coity Bach Self Catering Holiday
6 Forge Cottage
7 Gilestone Farm
8 Hawthorns, The
9 School Annex
10 Tiratanaloka Buddhist Retreat Centre
11 YHA Brecon Beacons Danywenalt

### 🚲 Bikes
1 Bikes & Hikes
2 Talybont Bike Hub

### ⛺ Camping
1 Talybont Farm Campsite

### Canal features
⚡ Charging point
⚓ Launch point
🌉 Lift bridge
🛏 Mooring
🗑 Rubbish
---- Towpath
💧 Waterpoint
🐚 Winding hole

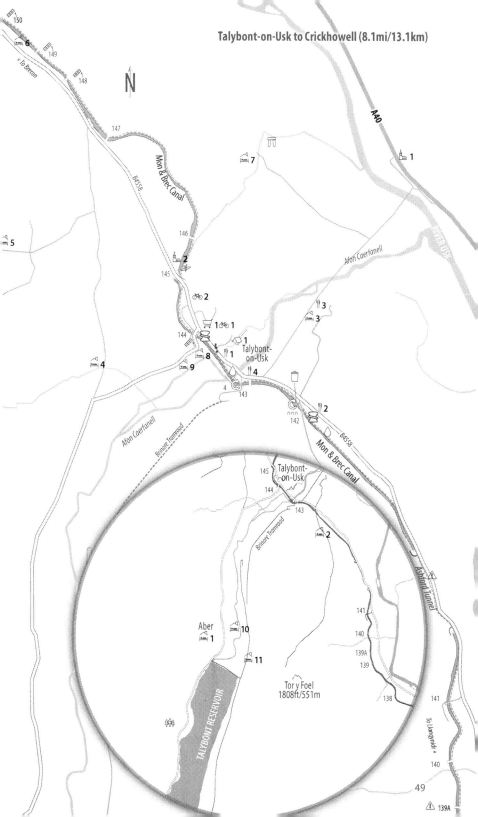

150
6
149
148
To Brecon
147
N
Mon & Brec Canal
B4558
146
5
145
2
2
144
1
1
8
4
4
9
143
4
4
1
1
Talybont-
on-Usk
3
3
Afon Caerfanell
A40
RIVER USK
1
7
142
2
B4558
Mon & Brec Canal
Afon Caerfanell
Brinore Tramroad
145
144
143
Talybont-
on-Usk
2
Brinore Tramroad
Ashford Tunnel
141
140
139A
139
138
141
Aber
1
10
11
Tor y Foel
1808ft/551m
TALYBONT RESERVOIR
To Llangynidr
140

139A

## Brecon Beacons National Park

This book is not meant to be a guide to the park, but it would be silly to ignore it considering that the Mon & Brec Canal is almost completely within the park. Of course much of what you'll want to see in the park will require a car, a bike or lots of shoe leather because the park covers 519 mi$^2$/1,340km$^2$ (about 44mi/71km wide by 22mi/35.5km tall and shaped liked Australia).

To Americans it doesn't seem like a national park because the Brecon Beacons encloses a mix of private land, commercial forests and mountains owned by the National Trust. The **national park** , established in 1957, is governed by a special purpose local authority that must negotiate all these interests. There are no entrance gates, no borders and no fee to enter the park. Several towns and villages, like Brecon and Crickhowell, are enclosed by the park.

The park is mostly grassy moorland punctuated by the Black Mountain in the west, the central beacons and the Black Mountains to the east (yes, Black Mountain *and* Black Mountains). Pen y Fan at 2,907ft/886m is the highest peak and the trail to the top is traveled by hundreds each day. Just left of center of the park and to the south is Fforest Fawr (Great Forest), which was a royal hunting park, and you'll find several waterfalls near Ystradfellte on the Four Falls Walk.

There are a number of castles in the park, the most impressive and picturesque being Carreg Cennen in the west. The park also includes a number of standing stones, Roman forts, tramroads, an abandoned

gunpowder works, quarries, an historic steam railway and of course the canal. Other natural wonders include the National Showcaves Centre near Black Mountain (the one in the west), Llangorse Lake, a number of reservoirs and the night sky (recognized by the park's International Dark Sky Reserve designation).

The park is crisscrossed by roads but many places in the park require some effort to access, like the National Park Visitor Centre. The **Beacons Way** Ⓦ, a 95mi/153km walking path, makes much of the park back country accessible. National Cycle Routes 8 and 42 also travel north to south through the park and there's a 58mi/93km east/west cycle route that follows a Roman road. One could easily spend a week in the park, hiking, spelunking, cycling, hang gliding and rock climbing, so plan to spend a week on the canal and a week in the rest of the park.

- **Tiratanaloka Buddhist Retreat Centre** Ⓦ
- **Yew Tree Cottage** Ⓦ
- **YHA Brecon Beacons Danywenalt** Ⓦ

## Camping/hostel

**Tal-y-bont Farm Caravan & Camping** Ⓦ , yet another family-run business, is on a working farm. For cyclists and hikers it offers toilets and showers. You'll need to call to book.

**Gilestone Farm** Ⓦ offers three luxury safari tents that can sleep up to six—more "glamping" than camping. There's also a self-catered farmhouse for hire and presumably farm guests will have access to the eponymous Giles Standing Stone.

Hikers, cyclists and those on a budget might enjoy staying at the YHA Brecon Beacons Danywenallt hostel at Talybont Reservoir. There's no upper age limit at the hostel and private en suite rooms are available.

*The view from Pen-y-fan, the highest mountain in the Brecon Beacons at 2,907ft/886m*

## Stores

**Talybont Stores, Cafe and Post Office** 🛈
sits just next to the canal. As well as
amenities such as Wi-Fi and public
toilets, it also offers packed lunch-
es as a convenience for hikers and
riders.

## Bike rental/services

**Bikes & Hikes** 🛈 *(see page 27)* is a bike
shop and bike hire just next door
to the Talybont stores. Just a little
north on the B4558 you can also
find the Talybont Bike Hub at Hen-
derson (village) Hall. The bike hub
offers a bike wash (£1 for 7 minutes),
bike repair stands and public toilet
(10p) and showers (£1).

## Biking and hiking

As mentioned earlier Talybont-on-Usk is ideally situated for hikers and
bikers of any fitness level. If you want to slow down, you might enjoy
the **Henry Vaughan Walk** 🛈 that follows the canal towpath, the Afon (afon
or avon means river) Caerfanell and abandoned tramroads. Henry and
his twin brother Thomas were respectively doctor and poet, and priest
and alchemist, born in 1621.

The walk is an easy 2.2mi/3.6km path best started at Bridge 143
on the canal towpath. Cross the bridge and walk southwest toward
the sadly neglected Vaughan Garden, a modern-day physic garden
emblematic of the herbs the brothers would have grown. Continue the
walk guided by signposts on which the brothers' poetry is reproduced.
You can also visit the grave of Henry Vaughan at **St. Ffraid** 🛈 on the
A40 just north of Talybont.

The walk follows the **Brinore Tramroad** 🛈 and then loops back to
Talybont following the Afon Caerfanell. If you want to sweat a little,
you could continue on the Brinore Tramroad to **Talybont Reservoir** 🛈.
The tramroad makes a loop on the east side of the reservoir (finished in
1939 to provide drinking water to Newport). The lime kilns just west
of Bridge 142 was the eventual destination of the limestone brought
down the tramroad. **My online maps** 🛈 will make these routes clear.

The western side of the reservoir is flanked by Talybont Forest, planted to prevent silt buildup in the water supply. It's a lovely
1.7mi/2.7km bike ride on the unnamed one-lane road to the reservoir,
although the view is often shrouded by trees. You can also cycle the
Brinore Tramroad to the reservoir, about 1.5mi/2.5km. Once you
reach the dam at the northern end of the reservoir, you'll be rewarded
by a magnificent view. From the canal, leave for the reservoir from
bridge 144, which is an electrically operated lift bridge.

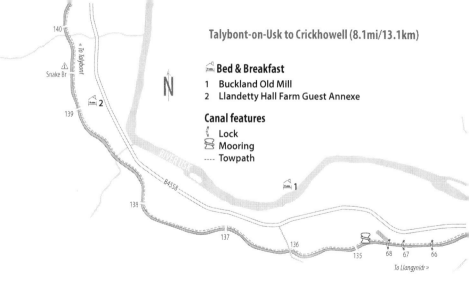

**Bed & Breakfast**
1   Buckland Old Mill
2   Llandetty Hall Farm Guest Annexe

**Canal features**
  Lock
  Mooring
---- Towpath

Boaters can raise bridge 144 with a Waterways key *(see page 27)*. Lower the bridge after passing.

There are several unusual lodging options near the reservoir, including a youth hostel, a women's spiritual retreat and a shepherd's hut. Unfortunately because it is a water supply there's no swimming or boating on the reservoir, but you can fish (except from the dam).

After Talybont, the canal continues its southeast course but about half a mile (833m) from bridge 142 you'll come to the 375-yard-long (0.2mi/0.3km) Ashford Tunnel. The tunnel is only wide enough for a single boat and as there is no towpath through the tunnel, hikers and cyclists will need to continue aboveground.

Since 2012, the Canal & River Trust has allowed canoeists to travel the Ashford Tunnel with the following requirements: Canoeists should first check the tunnel is clear of approaching boats and should have a flotation device, head lamp and whistle. Presumably stand up paddle boarders are under the same guidance.

Boaters should be aware that the ceiling height of the tunnel varies considerably. Take care not to get hit in the head. Anyone outside the cabin should wear a flotation device.

Of course boaters also have to take precautions traveling through tunnels. The tunnel must be clear of approaching boats, the horn must be sounded before entering and the headlight should be turned on. In addition the cabin should be illuminated and any open flames extinguished.

Because of the tunnel's low ceiling, boaters are advised to fill water tanks before traveling through the tunnel. Going south, bridge 142 is the last waterpoint before the tunnel.

Hikers and cyclists have an easy route over the tunnel. From Brecon, the towpath will merge with the B4558 about 600ft/183m from the north tunnel portal. However immediately after passing the north portal, you will see a footpath to the right (west) of the road. The footpath will take you through a sheep pasture. Cyclists, however, may want to remain on the B4558 depending on traffic. Heading north on the canal, the towpath continues past the south portal for 370ft/113m before either joining the B4558 or the footpath across the pasture.

The Ashford Tunnel is of cut-and-cover construction and there's a ventilation shaft about the halfway point. If your boat has bright lights and the water is still, you may notice the reflection of the tunnel ceiling on the water, giving the illusion that there is a deep, bricked channel under your boat.

After the excitement of the tunnel, the canal becomes very serene with not much of note apart from the beauty of the surrounding hills. Those vistas, however, will be replaced by another sort of tunnel—a tunnel of trees—a fairly common occurrence on most canals. Of

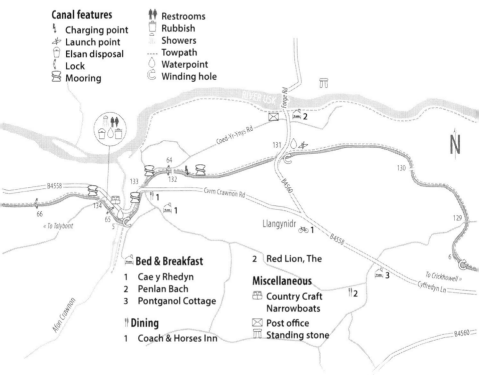

**Canal features**
- Charging point
- Launch point
- Elsan disposal
- Lock
- Mooring
- Restrooms
- Rubbish
- Showers
- Towpath
- Waterpoint
- Winding hole

**Bed & Breakfast**
1 Cae y Rhedyn
2 Penlan Bach
3 Pontganol Cottage

**Dining**
1 Coach & Horses Inn

2 Red Lion, The

**Miscellaneous**
Country Craft Narrowboats
Post office
Standing stone

*Negotiating the Llangynidr lock flight can be challenging, especially for beginners. Fortunately volunteer lockkeepers keep the process moving.*

course when the canals were first dug, they were largely stripped of trees but today on most canals it can be difficult to catch a glimpse of the countryside because much of the vegetation has grown back.

Travelers on the canal will also feel somewhat isolated on this stretch because the River Usk and the A40 are further north. There are bridges across the Usk and connecting with the A40 at Cefn Brynich and northeast of Talybont. The next bridge across the Usk won't be until Llangynidr.

Approaching Llangynidr the canal, the B4558 and the Usk head east as you approach the five-lock Llangynidr flight.

## Llangynidr

The Llangynidr flight includes five of the six locks on the canal and is a delightful experience thanks to the volunteer lockkeepers who keep traffic moving. The five locks are strung out about two-thirds of a mile (101m) and the last two locks are not visible from

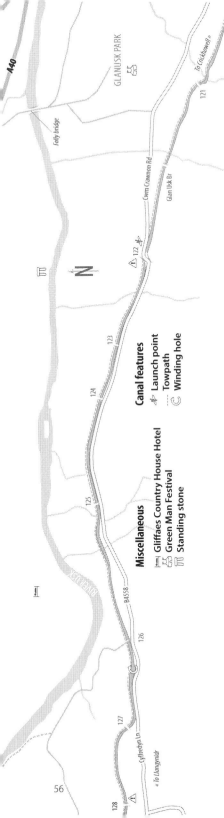

the first three. Follow the advice of the lockkeeper you're working with, even if that advice is different from the previous lockkeeper.

The locks on the canal are left empty after passage because the lock chambers leak badly and can swamp the surrounding soil

The locks aren't difficult to operate, but as usual care should be taken to avoid the cill when locking down (heading toward Abergavenny) and flooding the front of the boat when locking up (toward Brecon).

Especially when going up, the lockkeeper will advise you to slowly fill the lock chamber, opening only one of the ground paddles until your boat has cleared the cill. Remember to close the front doors of the boat when locking up.

During periods of low water supply the locks on the flight may be closed from 6 pm to 10 am

Incidentally, you're not supposed to moor overnight within a lock flight, but we and several other boats did with at least the tacit approval of the lockkeepers. The CRT map does show legal moorings within the flight.

The setting of the locks could not be more beautiful, especially lock 65 where you will find several Country Craft Narrowboats *(see page 27)* moored. You'll also find welcome services here such as restrooms and

showers. There's also a waterpoint that's essential if you're heading north to the Ashford Tunnel.

Look for the side pond on the north side of the top lock (number 68). This stores enough water to supply the flight.

There's a pleasant walk or bike ride on the south bank (non-towpath side) of the aqueduct that crosses the Afon Crawnon. The tree-shrouded path parallels that creek or river and also a feeder from the Crawnon that supplies the canal. The path ends at the weir that diverts the river into the feeder.

The aqueduct over the Crawnon is also where the Beacons Way crosses the canal and provides

**DANGER!** Beware the cill on the upstream gate of a lock. As a narrowboat descends the rear of the boat can be caught (as the water drains) on the stone or concrete cill against which the gate closes. The front of the boat can submerge and sink the boat. An ascending boat can also be caught by the upstream gate as the water rises. (NOTE: picture above is of a lock on the Llangollen Canal.)

another route to Tor y Foel. See the **online map** Ⓦ for details.

Unfortunately the **village of Llangynidr** Ⓦ (informally divided into Upper and Lower Llangynidr) has few diversions to offer. There's the Pepto-Bismol® pink **Coach & Horses Inn** Ⓦ just before the bottom lock; **The Red Lion Hotel** Ⓦ, slightly further in Lower Llangynidr (0.5mi/0.8km south of the canal from bridge 131); the **Church of St. Cyndir & St. Mary** Ⓦ; **Walnut Tree Stores** Ⓦ where you'll find groceries, a limited hours sub-post office and cafe; and Llangynidr Bridge, which carries Forge Road over the Usk.

The annual Llangynidr Duck Race is held at the Coach & Horses Bridge 133 in August. In 2019 first prize was a £200 voucher toward a boat hire with Road House Narrowboats.

The walk to the bridge is recommended and there are paths along the south bank of the Usk west and east of the bridge. There's also a standing stone or menhir on the north bank of the Usk, just east of the bridge. The **Gliffaes or Llwyn-y-Fedwen standing stone**  is one of the tallest Bronze Age stones in Wales, but unfortunately it sits in a private field. Ask the owners of Llwyn-y-Fedwen Farm for permission to view the stone (call or write in advance).

You'll sometimes be baffled by the purpose of some of the bridges over the canal as no roads lead to or away from them. These are accommodation bridges, meant to serve farmers whose fields have been divided by the canal.

With that we've exhausted the delights of Llangynidr and the canal continues east to Crickhowell. The canal remains close to the B4558 and the Usk but as usual the trees along the banks of the canal give the impression that you're in a world of your own.

In August, however, the sleepiness of the canal is awakened by the **Green Man Festival** on the **Glanusk Park** estate. Music, theater, film and poetry fans, up to 20,000, flock to multiple stages over four days. The rest of the year the 20,000-acre privately owned estate is quieter, offering self-catered cottages, an apartment in a wing of the main house and a caravan and camping park. There's also a "permissive" footpath to access a Victorian folly bridge[2] over the Usk.

The **Penmyarth or "Fish" standing stone** can also be found on the estate on the north bank of the Usk. Again you'd need to obtain permission before visiting.

If the permissive footpath through the Glanusk Estate is open, you'll find that's your easiest route from the canal by foot or bike (cyclists must dismount while on the path) to **Tretower Court**. After crossing the folly bridge, turn left onto the A40 and then follow an unmarked road to the court and castle. Originally a 12th-century motte-and-bailey castle, little remains of the later stone castle except part of the keep and surrounding wall. Fortunately a nearby 14th-century manor house favored by the lords of Tretower has been restored to its 1470 appearance.

---

2    Follies like the bridge and tower, were the architectural toys of the rich during the Georgian and Victorian eras

## Information & maps

 Talybont-on-Usk
Village
bit.ly/2Vdqm2C

 Llangynidr
Village
bit.ly/33lmOAh

 Llangynidr Local
History Society
bit.ly/2BVfijl

 Talybont
walk/cycle maps
bit.ly/2U1k0Hg

 Llangynidr
walk/cycle maps
bit.ly/2yOGVIT

 Brinore
Tramroad
bit.ly/2UZbVPZ

 Beacons
Way
bit.ly/2YaeWBG

 Brecon Beacons
National Park
bit.ly/2kBItma

## Attractions

 Henry Vaughan
Walk
bit.ly/2EacmQi

 St. Ffraid
Church
bit.ly/2TeDHKM

 Church of St. Cyndir
& St. Mary
bit.ly/2OPRzdu

 Talybont
Reservoir
bit.ly/2L8oBmn

 Tretower Court
and Castle
bit.ly/2xtpGvW

 Brinore
Tramroad
bit.ly/2tFfsHi

 Gliffaes
standing stone
bit.ly/2BUGX42

 Penmyarth "Fish"
standing stone
bit.ly/2tEaavx

 Glanusk
Park
bit.ly/2EhCpVw

## Festivals

 Talybont
Show
bit.ly/2G05ega

 Llangynidr
Agricultural Show
bit.ly/2T2Tqx9

 Over
the Baas
bit.ly/2H2AvLO

 Green Man
Festival
bit.ly/2GMWU02

## Lodging/Dining

*Talybont-on-Usk*

 The
Star Inn
bit.ly/2SYOKIK

 Travellers
Restaurant
bit.ly/2IDhxO0

 The
Usk Inn
bit.ly/2SsOPiC

 The
White Hart
bit.ly/2U6MrzB

*Llangynidr*

 Coach &
Horses Inn
bit.ly/2XlXG81

 The Red
Lion Hotel
bit.ly/2GXmK04

 Gliffaes Country
House Hotel
bit.ly/2YamilJ

## B&Bs/self-catering

*Talybont-on-Usk*

 Aber Farm
shepherd's hut
bit.ly/2IzNAhP

 Arches at
Baileys Barn
bit.ly/2XnBsnG

 Belvedere Bed
& Breakfast
bit.ly/2EaJaZy

 Cui Hen
Beudy Cottage
bit.ly/2SqDhMW

 Coity Bach Self
Catering Holiday
bit.ly/2H0x08x

 Old Forge
Cottage
bit.ly/2KqDdf4

 Gilestone
Farm
bit.ly/2NsxEgi

 The
Hawthorns
bit.ly/2IAtiEQ

 The School
Annex
bit.ly/2GKJ7HC

 Tiratanaloka
Buddhist Retreat
bit.ly/2ICjj1R

 YHA Brecon Beacons
Danywenalt
bit.ly/2GLkbPV

 Yew Tree
Cottage
bit.ly/2KFWUyp

*Llangynidr*

 Buckland
Old Mill
bit.ly/2IFDbiy

 Llandetty Hall Farm
Guest Annexe
bit.ly/2Y6YCOW

 Cae y Rhedyn
Annexe
bit.ly/2XtbaAv

 Penlan
Bach
bit.ly/2Y6Z7Zk

 Pontganol
Cottage
bit.ly/2ZI3v1k

## Camping

 Talybont Farm
Campsite
bit.ly/2T1XvBC

## Groceries/Cafe

 Talybont Stores
Cafe and Post Office
bit.ly/2U6MYBD

 Walnut Tree
Stores Llangynidr
bit.ly/2XnKGA5

## Bikes

 Talybont
Bike Hub
bit.ly/2XnEwzZ

*You'll find many examples of canal "furniture" scattered along the canal. These planks at the Llangynidr lock flight can be dropped into slots in the canal to hold back water for inspections or repairs. Also look for the plug on the Brynich Aqueduct.*

*View of Crickhowell from the remains of Crickhowell Castle*

# Crickhowell to Abergavenny
(6.8mi/11km)[1]

From Crickhowell to Abergavenny you're traveling the heart of the Monmouthshire & Brecon Canal. The canal has a brooding, claustrophobic aspect caused by the steep slope on the southern (or western) bank and by the trees that almost deny any glimpse of sky or view. I call these Heart of Darkness or African Queen moments where the putt-putt-putt of the boat and the unchanging scenery make it seem as if you have no progress.

The towns of Crickhowell and Abergavenny and the village of Gilwern, however, are welcome reminders of civilization. Even Gilwern, which is not very picturesque, is worth a visit and Crickhowell is, in my opinion, the most attractive town or village on the canal. The bridge across the Usk to Crickhowell is impressive and the buildings, as in Brecon, are either whitewashed or sport pastel hues and are mostly Georgian. It's a lovely town to walk because the A4077 keeps much of the traffic away from the High Street (although the A40 does bisect the town).

---

1   To Tod's Bridge/Llanfoist Wharf

# The Monmouthshire & Brecon Canal

HERONS REST MARINA

To Gilwern

110

111

112

113

Great Oak Rd

Bellfountain Rd

12

CRICKHOWELL

Castle Rd

Llanbedr Rd

3

A40

9

2

2

High St

2

Bridge St

A4077

2

A4077

8

Hillside Rd

5

4

1

N

4

Cwm Crawnon Rd

1

5

Llangattock

114

115

1

4

7

116

117

13

118

5

119

5

Beaufort St

4

Stanhope St

2

3

1

RIVER USK

B4558

Mon & Brec Canal

To Llangynidr

120

A40

3

2

8

4

1

2

12

3

3

2

1

4

1

1

3

2

3

6

High St

Castle Rd

1

11

10,14

13

1

2

A4077

4

62

## Attractions

⬜ Crickhowell Castle
~~~ Llangattock Lime Kilns
🌲 Giant Sequoia

## ⛪ Churches

1 St. Catwg
2 St. Edwards Church

## 🏨 Hotels

1 Bear Hotel, The
2 Bridge End Inn, The
3 Dragon Inn, The
4 Horseshoe Inn, The
5 Old Rectory, The

## 🏠 Bed & Breakfast

1 Bridge House
2 Crickhowell Cottage
3 Glan y Dwr Bed & Breakfast
4 Gwyn Deri Bed & Breakfast
5 Merryfields Barn
6 Mortimer House
7 The Neuadd Cottages and B&B Suites
8 Park Place Guest House
9 Porth Y Berllan Bed & Breakfast
10 Ramblers Rest Cottage
11 Steps Cottage
12 Studio, The
13 Ty Croeso B & B
14 No. 14 Bridge Street Holiday Cottage

## 🏕 Camping

1 Park Farm
2 Riverside Caravan Park

## 🍴 Pubs/Restaurants

1 Britannia Inn
2 Beaufort, The
3 Swan Inn, The
4 Red Indigo
5 Vine Tree, The

## ☕ Cafe

1 Askew's
2 Courtroom Cafe, The
3 Latte–da Coffee & Kitchen
4 Pantry Coffeehouse & Brunchery, The

## 🍟 Fast food

1 Wok Experience
2 Yummy Kitchen

## 🛒 Groceries

1 Cashells
2 Grenfells & Sons Grocers
3 Jehu's Stores
4 FE Richards

## 🛍 Shopping

1 Corn Exchange, The

2 Crickhowell Adventure
3 Nicholls

## Miscellaneous

⬜ Beacon Park Boats
⬜ Bookish
⬜ Boots
? Crickhowell Resource & Information Centre
⬜ Crickhowell Police Station

## Canal features

🗑 Elsan disposal
⚓ Launch point
⬜ Lock
⬜ Mooring
⬜ Restrooms
⬜ Rubbish
⬜ Showers
┊ Towpath
◇ Waterpoint
🔄 Winding hole

The lime kilns at Llangattock south of Crickhowell are well preserved and you'll also find CRT facilities here

Lime kilns and canals go together. Crushed limestone was often transported to canals via tramways and the kilns were built next to the canal. This meant the processed lime could be directly loaded onto boats. The lime was also used as some of the mortar on the stone and brick work of the canal.

## Crickhowell

Crickhowell is a market town of more than 2,000 people, although various events like the Green Man Festival boost that number. The name is an Anglicized version of the nearby Iron Age Crug Hywel hill fort atop Table Mountain. With its many hotels, pubs, B&Bs and shops, the town rivals Brecon and Abergavenny for convenience. In fact in 2018 Crickhowell was named best in the Great British High Street Awards.

As the canal approaches Crickhowell it shies away and loops south toward the village of Llangattock. The Usk, however, continues and marks the southern edge of Crickhowell. As a consequence, if you want to visit Crickhowell from the canal on foot, you're in for a long walk. It's best to moor near Dan-Y-Garth Bridge 115 or Ffawyddog

Bridge 116. From Bridge 116 it's about 0.62mi/1km to get to The Bridge End Inn and from Bridge 115 about 0.87mi/1.4km.

## Information

The Crickhowell Resource & Information Centre on Beaufort Street is a great place to stop for maps, books and souvenirs. Visit the **CRiC website** Ⓦ before your trip as well.

## Attractions

**Crickhowell (or Alisby's) Castle** Ⓦ was originally a motte-and-bailey (raised earthwork surrounded by a ditch or wall) castle built by the Turberville family in the 12th century, and then rebuilt in stone in 1272. The castle's crumbling walls overlook a playground and the nearby remains of the original motte give a fine view of the Usk Valley.

The **Llangattock Lime Kilns** Ⓦ are remarkably well preserved and the characteristic arches sit just next to the canal (for easy loading onto barges) at bridge 115. You'll also find CRT services like restrooms and showers here.

Definitely take the time to explore the lime kilns. There are picnic tables to enjoy the view above the kilns and you'll also see that one of the pits remains unfilled. You can also peer through the arches of the kiln and see where the processed lime was removed.

The 18th-century Crickhowell Bridge over the Usk is the longest stone bridge in Wales and has the peculiarity that it has 12 arches on one side and 13 on the other. The weir below the bridge adds to its appeal.

## Festivals

The **Crickhowell Walking Festival** Ⓦ in March offers nine days of guided (ticketed) walks in the Black Mountains. The **Crickhowell Music Festival** Ⓦ combines five days of bluegrass and classical music in May. In August the nearby Green Man Festival *(see page 59)* also draws music lovers. And in late September-early October you can enjoy the **Crickhowell Literary Festival** Ⓦ.

## Lodging

Crickhowell has several hotels and a really impressive number of B&Bs and self-catered cottages. The Old Rectory Hotel in Llangattock, which looks like a locale from an Agatha Christie movie, is very convenient to the canal. It has a range of rooms from singles and double to family rooms, an executive suite and a honeymoon suite. It's dog friendly but with a £5 surcharge per night. There's plenty of parking and even a nine-hole golf course. Oh, and remember the footpath dedicated to Henry Vaughan and his brother at Talybont-on-Usk? Henry was the rector of Llangattock and lived in what is now **The Old Rectory Hotel** Ⓦ.

**The Bear Hotel** Ⓦ is a former coaching inn and has 35 rooms (some accessible). The building dates to 1432 and despite additions still looks quite historic. It has pride of place at the end of the High Street in Crickhowell as well as free parking. Dogs stay free.

The 23-room **Manor Hotel** ⓦ (not shown on the map) was a Georgian manor house and possibly the birthplace of Sir George Everest, for whom the world's tallest peak is named. The hotel is off the A40 as it approaches Crickhowell from the west. There is free parking and an indoor pool. You can book room only, B&B or B&B plus dinner.

Dating from the 1500s, the 15-room **Dragon Inn** ⓦ sits on the High Street. We found the service prompt and I had a satisfying cream tea here and an introduction to Welsh cakes. Dogs are welcome in certain rooms at a £15 surcharge. Breakfast is included, parking is free and electric vehicle charging is provided.

The **Bridge End Inn** ⓦ sits on the northern bank of the Usk and has the best view of the bridge from its beer garden. The inn, which used to be a toll house, has a double, double en suite and a cottage to let. There's also a car park.

The **Horseshoe Inn** ⓦ, an early 19th-century coaching inn in Llangattock, is also convenient to the canal and has five rooms. Breakfast and free parking is included. It's very dog friendly.

There are too many B&Bs or self-catered accommodations in and around Crickhowell to list here although you'll find links at the end of the chapter. **Ty Croeso B&B** ⓦ is the most convenient to the canal just

at bridge 118. Many can be found along the A4077, the main road that crosses the Crickhowell Bridge, or the parallel Bridge Street.

## Camping

You'll find two caravan parks, **Riverside Caravan Park** and **Park Farm** ⓦ. The first is convenient to Crickhowell and offers toilets, showers, laundry room, Wi-Fi water and electric. It's also adults only. Park Farm is convenient to Llangattock and offers toilets, showers, electricity, cooking facilities and a farm shop.

## Shopping

Most of the shopping found in Crickhowell is of the local variety, but there is a small **Nicholls** ⓦ department store (useful for US visitors who arrived without a flannel for their face) on the High Street. You'll also find the recently opened **Corn Exchange** ⓦ and the bookstore **Bookish** ⓦ on the High Street.

## Groceries

Local groceries (and butchers) are also located on the High Street including **Grenfell's & Sons Grocers** ⓦ, **Cashells Butchers and Delicatessen** ⓦ (which stepped up to the plate when I asked for a cheddar so sharp it would knock my socks off) and **FE Richards High-Class Butchers** ⓦ. I've also listed several cafés that are also bakeries (or *vice versa*). **Jehu's Stores** ⓦ, where generations of school children have bought sweets, can also be found near the intersection of the High Street and A40.

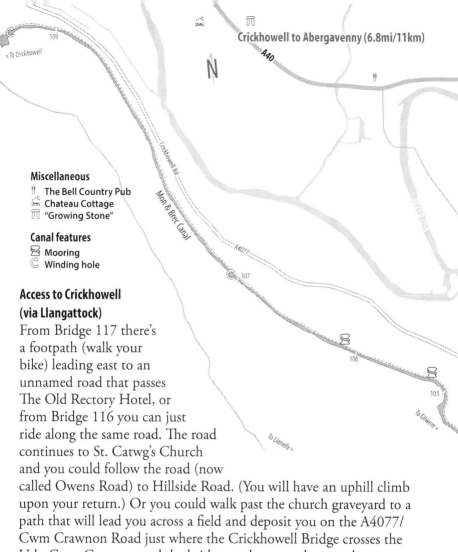

**Miscellaneous**

¶ The Bell Country Pub
🏠 Chateau Cottage
🎏 "Growing Stone"

**Canal features**

🐚 Mooring
Ͼ Winding hole

## Access to Crickhowell (via Llangattock)

From Bridge 117 there's a footpath (walk your bike) leading east to an unnamed road that passes The Old Rectory Hotel, or from Bridge 116 you can just ride along the same road. The road continues to St. Catwg's Church and you could follow the road (now called Owens Road) to Hillside Road. (You will have an uphill climb upon your return.) Or you could walk past the church graveyard to a path that will lead you across a field and deposit you on the A4077/ Cwm Crawnon Road just where the Crickhowell Bridge crosses the Usk. Cwm Crawnon and the bridge road are very busy and cars are let across the one-lane bridge by alternating traffic signals. The wide sidewalk is on the north side of the bridge. Cross the bridge and you've passed from Llangattock to Crickhowell. It's about 0.6mi/0.96km from Bridge 115 to Bridge End Inn on the other side of the Usk.

St. Catwg's Church is sufficiently quaint and has a long history, founded in the 6th century by St. Catwg (or Cadog), although the present church dates to the 1100s. The Welsh name for Llangattock incidentally is Llangatwg and the saint is said to have been baptized in the Nant Onneu that runs next to the church.

You can also access Crickhowell from (Upper Yard) Bridge 115 or (Lower Yard) Bridge 114, but it's a longer walk on Hillside Road to

Crickhowell. However it's a much more convenient path on a bike and is an easy ride. Hillside Road will take you past The Horseshoe Inn and **The Vine Tree** Ⓦ.

Although Crickhowell is a delightful town to wander (my **online map** Ⓦ shows the route), Table Mountain to the north and Llangattock Escarpment to the south of Crickhowell beckons walkers and cyclists.

### Crug Hywel

There's little to see of the Iron Age fort on Crug Hywel/Table Mountain, but the views are spectacular. Hikers and cyclists can either approach the fort from the north and west or more directly from the south or combine both routes to make a loop. Unfortunately cyclists should dismount on Table Mountain Path.

For cyclists starting from the lime kilns, it's a 3mi/4.8km route to the fort with 1,300ft/396m of elevation change. The most direct route once you've made it to Crickhowell is to follow Llanbedr Road northeast from the A40, and then north onto Table Mountain Path at a farm house. You could probably walk your bike to the fort but it would make more sense to lock it up before taking the path.

An alternate route once across Crickhowell Bridge is to follow the A4077 until turning left at the A40. Follow the A40 northwest to an unnamed road (unfortunately a narrow one lane with no shoulder or sidewalk) that runs northeast. Follow the unnamed road for 780ft/238m until you see a path that leads to Table Mountain Path. The path leads north of the

N

Crug Hywel
1,480 ft/451 m

Table Mountain Path

Table Mountain Path

A40

← To Crickhowell

Llanbedr Rd

Great Oak Rd

fort and then turns south to the summit. You can follow these routes on my **online map** ⬦.

This route is 3.5mi/5.6km and has 1,431ft/436m of elevation change. You could retrace your steps back or make a 6.6mi/10.6km loop, returning to Crickhowell via the Llanbedr Road route previously described. Personally I think the Llanbedr Road route is more bike friendly although it does become an unnamed one-lane narrow road just before Table Mountain Path.

*West of Bridge 113 (east of Llangattock) you'll be surprised to see on the towpath side this giant sequoia, measured in 2009 at 129.6ft/39.5m tall*

You can slightly modify the Llanbedr route and instead follow Great Oak Road, which will meet Llanbedr Road on the way to Crug Hywel. The Great Oak standing stone is near the intersection of Great Oak and Bellfountain roads. I don't know if it's possible to access the stone or see it from the road and yes, I realize this is an essentially useless bit of information.

## Llangattock Escarpment

South of the canal from Crickhowell is Mynydd Llangatwg (Llangattock Mountain), the most prominent feature of which is the Llangattock Escarpment. The cliff face of the escarpment offers a great view of the Usk Valley and Llangattock and Crickhowell. You can follow the edge of the escarpment to abandoned limestone quarries (that fed the Llangattock lime kilns). This is an otherworldly landscape dotted with small hillocks and pockmarked by shake holes. It's a 1.8mi/2.9km hike or bike ride and a 771ft/235m elevation gain along a one-lane road from bridge 114 to the quarry car park.

There are also extensive caves along the escarpment and three cave systems are accessible, but you'll need to contact a local caving group to explore them. Parts of the escarpment are protected as the Craig y Cilau National Nature Reserve due to the number of plant species found here.

After Llangattock, the canal will pass by Beacon Park Boats and then shortly after Herons Rest Marina. After the marina the canal, the A4077 (now called Crickhowell Road) and the Usk meet again until the Usk veers north of Gilwern.

As mentioned earlier, the canal is dark and mysterious here, heavily wooded with Douglas fir, larch and hemlock. The western (or southern bank) rises sharply further increasing the brooding atmosphere.

## Gilwern

Perhaps not the most attractive village on the canal, Gilwern is nevertheless welcome after the canal's dark passage. It's home to two boat hires, several pubs, a grocery store, butchers and B&Bs. It also has the scariest CRT services on the canal, but more on that later.

 Unlike many of the standing stones previously mentioned, the Growing Stone, northwest of Gilwern, is easily visible from the A40. Even though it's on Ministry of Defence property, a sidewalk is just 100ft/30.5m away.

You'll encounter Castle Narrowboats *(see page 27)* first just before the aqueduct that carries the canal over the River Clydach and then Road House Narrowboats where Main Road (A4077) crosses the canal. Main Road, which I think is the high street, also leads south to the still under construction A465 or Heads of the Valley Road. The improved A465 will be a split-level carriageway following the River Clydach to Brynmawr. The Gateway Bridge over the Clydach Gorge opened in 2018 and A465 construction is expected to be completed in 2019.

### Lodging

The **Beaufort Arms B&B** Ⓦ is a surprisingly nice spot to eat or stay. It has three rooms and definitely has the feel of a place where the locals eat and drink … although it's not like there are many alternatives.

For a while **The Corn Exchange** Ⓦ (on the A4077 as it approaches Gilwern) was the only other pub in Gilwern, The Navigation and Bridgend Inn just by the canal having closed. The Bridgend, however, has reopened as the **Towpath Inn** Ⓦ and is styled as a pub/coffee shop.

Other accommodations include **Mill-Lodge Brecon Beacons** and **The Old Stable** Ⓦ and even Road House

## Canal features
- ⚡ Charging point
- 🚽 Elsan disposal
- ⚓ Launch point

- Lime kilns
- Mooring
- Pump out
- Restrooms

- 🚿 Showers
- ---- Towpath
- Waterpoint
- ℃ Winding hole

Gilwern    Mon & Brec Canal

### B&B
1 Courtyard Cottage
2 Llanwenarth Cottage
3 Mill-Lodge Brecon Beacons
4 Old Stable, The

### Dining
1 Beaufort Arms, The
2 Corn Exchange, The

3 Towpath Inn

### Boat hire
1 Castle Narrowboats
2 Road House Narrowboats

### Groceries
1 Bromfields Butchers
2 Gilwern Stores

3 SPAR Gilwern
4 Londis

### Miscellaneous
- John Willams
- Village Fish Bar
- Hopyard Cycles

---

Narrowboats has a room to let. Mill-Lodge is unique in that it offers photography training and guided photo tours.

## Groceries

A short walk up Church Road from Bridge 104 will take you to both the **SPAR** and **One Stop** small groceries on the A4077 (Crickhowell Road). Walk north from Bridge 103 on Main Road and you'll find the small **Londis** grocery store. Or shop locally at **Bromfields Purveyors of Quality Meats** also on Main Road. In addition to meat you can also buy (meat) pies, eggs and something scarily called Irish Curry Sauce.

## CRT services

One of Gilwern's dubious distinctions is that here you'll find the scariest services on the canal. Having cycled CRT canals, I really appreciate finding a toilet that doesn't require me to buy something at a store or stop at a pub. And even when traveling on a narrowboat, I occasionally enjoy taking a shower at a CRT service, rather than dealing with a cramped, swaying, onboard shower stall.

You'll find Beaufort in the names of towns, pubs and companies along the canal, a reference to the Dukes of Beaufort. The sixth duke was an investor in the Brecknock & Abergavenny Canal and the family remains large landowners.

Now even at the best of times CRT services can be grim, but the four stalls dug into the side of the embankment above Gilwern Wharf *(see page 17)* look post-apocalyptic. One door was wide open and the interior devastated and another door couldn't be opened. Perhaps during daylight I would have chanced a shower, but it was too scary to use at night. You might want to wait until the services at Govilon.

The embankment into which the toilets are dug is interesting, however. The 80ft/24m hill was built to carry the canal in an aqueduct over the River Clydach and emphasizes just how important Gilwern was during the Industrial Revolution. The embankment is one of the largest earthworks on a Welsh canal, but trees obscure the achievement. The embankment is also pierced by a railway tunnel.

Heading south from the wharf the canal encounters Bridge 103, which is clearly very low, and hides an exposed pipe halfway through. Heed the warning signs and if necessary top off your water tank before entering.

 The towpath leading up from the north bank of bridge 103 is the route into Gilwern and will take you to Road House Narrowboats and its well-stocked gift shop. Well worth a visit as is the rest of Gilwern despite my snarky comments.

Poor Gilwern is further disfigured by the A465 bridge over the canal. We spotted the canal's one and only example of graffiti (that I observed) while passing under the bridge. Once through the bridge the canal briefly parallels the motorway before leaving it. The countryside is unexpectedly pretty in this short stretch between Gilwern and Govilon, but that makes sense because the canal passes just north of Llanwenarth House. Supposedly Cecil Frances Alexander wrote the hymn *All Things Bright and Beautiful* while a guest at the house. Or maybe she wrote it elsewhere; regardless Llanwenarth House is just south of the canal at Bridge 100 and it would be tempting to visit. Don't—although it had been a hotel it is now private property.

North of the canal and the A465 you'll find Hopyard Cycles and Courtyard Cottage *(see page 27)*. The latter can accommodate up to 14 guests, so it might be a great spot for a large cycling party to explore the canal.

## Govilon

Just before arriving in Abergavenny you'll find Govilon Wharf. Quite often on a narrowboat it can be quite tedious slowly passing moored boats but the canal next to the wharf is very pretty and the houses next to the water are delightful as well. Keep an eye out for the skewed 97A railway bridge with its distinctive brickwork. The old canal warehouse at the wharf is now the Canal & River Trust offices with services

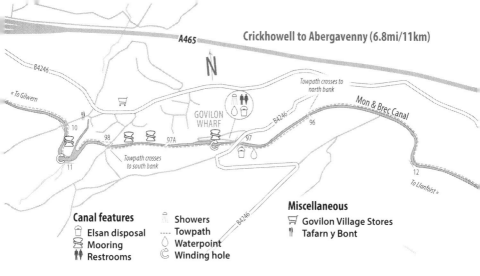

**Crickhowell to Abergavenny (6.8mi/11km)**

**Canal features**
- Elsan disposal
- Mooring
- Restrooms
- Showers
- Towpath
- Waterpoint
- Winding hole

**Miscellaneous**
- Govilon Village Stores
- Tafarn y Bont

including restrooms and showers. There's also a village store and pub nearby.

### Clydach Gorge and Blaenavon

Govilon, by the way, makes a good starting point for cyclists wishing to see the Clydach Gorge or the Blaenavon Industrial World Heritage Site. From the wharf take NCR 46 west. The cycle route will parallel the A465 but at a comfortable distance and lead to Clydach and the Gorge.

The area will be of interest to students of the industrial revolution as the cycle route follows the path of the abandoned Merthyr, Tredegar and Abergavenny Railway. You'll ride over viaducts and see lime kilns, ironworks and tramroads. Despite the proximity of the A465 it's still majestic. If you go down to the River Clydach you can enjoy gorge scrambling up the many waterfalls, although you will get wet and some technical climbing is involved. **Inspire2Adventure** ⓦ offers group scrambles.

After Clydach, NCR 46 intersects with NCR 492. Turn left or east to Blaenavon, or for a slightly shorter route leave NCR 46 where it intersects with Station Road and take an unnamed road to Blaenavon. Unfortunately you'll miss seeing Clydach Gorge if you leave the national cycle route, but you could add a side trip to the summit of The Blorenge.

Blaenavon, for a town of 6,000, has a lot to offer including **The Big Pit National Coal Museum**, the **Blaenavon World Heritage Centre**, the **Blaenavon Ironworks** and the **Pontypool and Blaenavon Railway** ⓦ. There's also a wealth of pubs, hotels and B&Bs in the area. It's well worth a visit but for canal travelers without a bike it's too far by foot. I have created **an online map** ⓦ for the gorge and Blaenavon.

## Information

 Visit
Crickhowell
bit.ly/2WwPrq3

 Crickhowell walk/
cycle maps
bit.ly/2TWYjYU

 Blaenavon walk/
cycle maps
bit.ly/2Oqd2px

 Govilon
Village website
bit.ly/2REiOp1

## Attractions

 Crickhowell
Castle
bit.ly/2YteNH2

 Llangattock Lime
Kilns
bit.ly/2JGPnSV

 Crug
Hywel
bit.ly/2OxRnM8

 St. Catwg
bit.ly/2YvCZZa

 Clydach
Gorge
bit.ly/2NDPoJo

 Inspire2Adventure
bit.ly/2XVepQb

 Big Pit National
Coal Museum
bit.ly/2XVjesK

 Blaenavon World
Heritage Centre
bit.ly/30DPzGe

 Blaenavon
Ironworks
bit.ly/2xR7r3M

 Pontypool and
Blaenavon Railway
bit.ly/2Oa8nLY

## Festivals

 Crickhowell Walking
Festival
bit.ly/2TsjEG5

 Crickhowell Music
Festival
bit.ly/2U3kPzB

 Crickhowell Literary
Festival
bit.ly/2TDmy9y

## Lodging/Dining

*Crickhowell*

 The Bear
Hotel
bit.ly/2TYnwCp

 The Bridge
End Inn
bit.ly/2FEKqWA

*Looking north up the High Street in Crickhowell*

The
Dragon Inn
bit.ly/2WroP9I

 The
Horseshoe
bit.ly/2FEOm9Z

The Old
Rectory
bit.ly/2uxxqMg

Manor
Hotel
bit.ly/2Tsgi6g

*Gilwern*

 The Beaufort
Arms
bit.ly/2YIrL3B

 The
Corn Exchange
bit.ly/2YPN3ey

Towpath
Inn
bit.ly/2CPurTR

## Pubs

*Crickhowell*

Britannia
Inn
bit.ly/2TGYWkz

The Swan
Inn
bit.ly/2CI21Lg

Red
Indigo
bit.ly/2TCL0I5

 The Vine
Tree
bit.ly/2Fx251c

*Gilwern*

 The Corn
Exchange
bit.ly/2YPN3ey

*Govilon*

 Tafarn
y Bont
bit.ly/2FvVWmR

## Cafés

*Crickhowell*

 Askew's
Bakery
bit.ly/2JYaHDq

The Courtroom
Cafe
bit.ly/2HShzk2

Latte-da Coffee &
Kitchen
bit.ly/2FOZe54

Pantry Coffeehouse
& Brunchery
bit.ly/2JYcit9

## Takeaway

*Crickhowell*

 Wok
Experience
bit.ly/2xBlri2

Yummy
Kitchen
bit.ly/2FO9rNQ

*Gilwern*

 Village
Fish Bar
bit.ly/2WJgUox

## B&Bs/self-catering

*Crickhowell*

 Bridge
House
bit.ly/2JG5Nea

 Crickhowell
Cottage
bit.ly/2FEU7Es

Glan y Dwr Bed &
Breakfast
bit.ly/2KkNEkg

Gwyn Deri Bed &
Breakfast
bit.ly/2Ua7Jjj

Merryfields
Barn
bit.ly/2YuiP1W

Mortimer
House
bit.ly/2JMbFCT

 Neuadd Cottages
and B&B Suites
bit.ly/2U3aLX4

Park Place Guest
House
bit.ly/2uyrFxE

 Porth Y Berllan Bed
& Breakfast
bit.ly/2JHGnwM

 Ramblers Rest
Cottage
bit.ly/2Fvy55J

 Steps
Cottage
bit.ly/2TYLCgl

 The
Studio
bit.ly/2WvQqqp

 Ty Croeso
B & B
bit.ly/2HWUZpu

 No. 14 Bridge Street
Holiday Cottage
bit.ly/2OuofFo

*Gilwern*

 Courtyard
Cottage
bit.ly/2U8ug06

 Llanwenarth
Cottage
bit.ly/2Va7mCn

 Mill-Lodge
Brecon Beacons
bit.ly/2HTHuYp

 The Old
Stable
bit.ly/2KaR63h

## Camping

Park
Farm
bit.ly/2HKjhUw

 Riverside
Caravan Park
bit.ly/2UiB8Yt

## Groceries

*Crickhowell*

 Cashells Butchers &
Delicatessen
bit.ly/2YFMTaS

 Grenfells & Sons
Grocers
bit.ly/2UoGykM

 FE Richards
High-Class Butchers
bit.ly/33sSOSP

 Jehu's
Store
bit.ly/2KsBtC0

*Gilwern*

 Bromfields
Butchers
bit.ly/2I3Dy6N

 One
Stop
bit.ly/2TPwvRx

 Londis
Gilwern
bit.ly/2WE4E8u

 SPAR
Gilwern
bit.ly/2FK7m5K

*Govilon*

 Govilon
Village Store
bit.ly/2CNP4jg

## Shopping

*Crickhowell*

 Bookish
bit.ly/33nEgEa

 The Corn
Exchange
bit.ly/2KENXFG

 Crickhowell
Adventure
bit.ly/2TFujvB

 Nicholls
Crickhowell
bit.ly/2TZSOJ7

## Pharmacy

*Crickhowell*

 Boots
Pharmacy
bit.ly/2NsxAk9

*Gilwern*

 John Williams
Pharmacy
bit.ly/2HSB3Ff

## Taxis

 CTE Crickhowell
Taxis
bit.ly/2HViAb4

 Grab a Cab
Crickhowell
bit.ly/2VeoRSa

Town to Town
1873 812399

*Cattle greet you as you walk the paths of Castle Meadows below Abergavenny. It's a pleasant walk beside the river ... some recompense for having survived "The Bridge of Death."*

# Abergavenny to Goytre Wharf
(5.7mi/9.1km)[1]

The canal from Abergavenny to Goytre Wharf starts off with a bang at Abergavenny, the largest town on the realistically navigable portion of the canal. Then the canal becomes extremely pastoral, bucolic and soporific. Perversely it also becomes challenging for narrowboaters with tight turns, low bridges and the horrible sound of your hull scraping the bottom.

Cyclists, however, should really enjoy the towpath except for the lack of public restrooms until Goytre Wharf. This coupled with the lack of canal-side pubs will lend a certain urgency to your pace. Hikers, of course, will probably find the lack of toilets even more challenging—a challenge intensified by the open countryside. After leaving The Blorenge behind, the canal is in flatter country flanked by open fields, and thus it's difficult to make like a bear in the woods. Nevertheless boaters, cyclists and hikers should enjoy this stretch of the canal.

## Abergavenny

Abergavenny (literally the mouth of the River Gafenni) has the most right to call itself a market town, with general markets three days a

1    To Goytre Aqueduct No. 15

ABERGAVENNY

A40

A40

A4233

King St

Lion St

Market St

Lydd St

Queen St

High St

Nevill St

Castle St

Bakers St

Victoria St

Tudor St

Merthyr Rd

Merthyr Rd

RIVER USK

The Cutting

A4143

A465

N

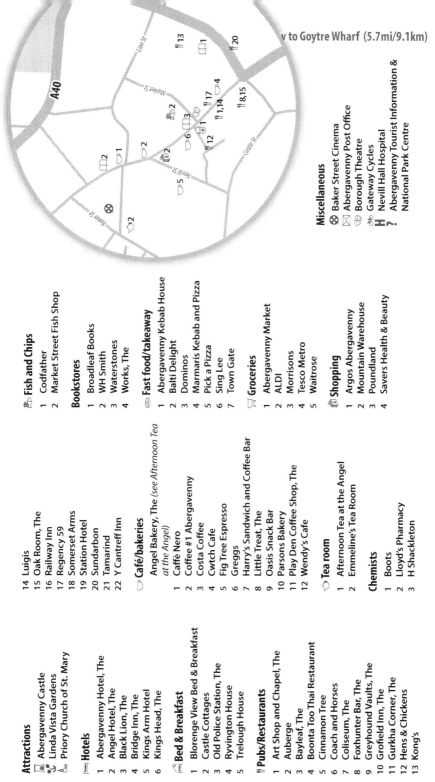

to Goytre Wharf (5.7mi/9.1km)

**Attractions**
Abergavenny Castle
Linda Vista Gardens
Priory Church of St. Mary

**Hotels**
1 Abergavenny Hotel, The
2 Angel Hotel, The
3 Black Lion, The
4 Bridge Inn, The
5 Kings Arm Hotel
6 Kings Head, The

**Bed & Breakfast**
1 Blorenge View Bed & Breakfast
2 Castle Cottages
3 Old Police Station, The
4 Ryvington House
5 Trelough House

**Pubs/Restaurants**
1 Art Shop and Chapel, The
2 Auberge
3 Bayleaf, The
4 Boonta Too Thai Restaurant
5 Cinnamon Tree
6 Coach and Horses
7 Coliseum, The
8 Foxhunter Bar, The
9 Greyhound Vaults, The
10 Grofeld Inn, The
11 Gurkha Corner, The
12 Hens & Chickens
13 Kong's
14 Luigis
15 Oak Room, The
16 Railway Inn
17 Regency 59
18 Somerset Arms
19 Station Hotel
20 Sundarbon
21 Tamarind
22 Y Cantreff Inn

**Café/bakeries**
Angel Bakery, The (see Afternoon Tea at the Angel)
1 Caffè Nero
2 Coffee #1 Abergavenny
3 Costa Coffee
4 Cwtch Cafe
5 Fig Tree Espresso
6 Greggs
7 Harry's Sandwich and Coffee Bar
8 Little Treat, The
9 Oasis Snack Bar
10 Parsons Bakery
11 Play Den Coffee Shop, The
12 Wendy's Cafe

**Tea room**
1 Afternoon Tea at the Angel
2 Emmeline's Tea Room

**Chemists**
1 Boots
2 Lloyd's Pharmacy
3 H Shackleton

**Fish and Chips**
1 Codfather
2 Market Street Fish Shop

**Bookstores**
1 Broadleaf Books
2 WH Smith
3 Waterstones
4 Works, The

**Fast food/takeaway**
1 Abergavenny Kebab House
2 Balti Delight
3 Dominos
4 Marmaris Kebab and Pizza
5 Pick a Pizza
6 Sing Lee
7 Town Gate

**Groceries**
1 Abergavenny Market
2 ALDI
3 Morrisons
4 Tesco Metro
5 Waitrose

**Shopping**
1 Argos Abergavenny
2 Mountain Warehouse
3 Poundland
4 Savers Health & Beauty

**Miscellaneous**
Baker Street Cinema
Abergavenny Post Office
Borough Theatre
Gateway Cycles
Nevill Hall Hospital
Abergavenny Tourist Information & National Park Centre

79

*Abergavenny Market*

week and additional flea market, craft fair, antique fair and artisan days throughout the month. And as a town of 12,000, you'll find plenty of shops, restaurants, hotels and B&Bs. Other attractions include Abergavenny Castle, Linda Vista Gardens, St. Mary's Priory Church and … the bridge of death.

OK, that last is a slight exaggeration, but to be honest getting from the canal to Abergavenny involves both toil and danger. From Tod's Bridge 95A it's 0.8mi/1.3km just to get to Abergavenny Bridge and there is a steep descent from the canal. It's not enough to tax anyone reasonably fit, but if you've already been riding a bike or hiking for several days previous to this, it's a climb you're not looking forward to on your return, especially if laden with groceries or souvenirs.

The danger comes from crossing the bridge over the Usk, especially if you're on the wrong side of the street. Although at first glance this Tudor bridge (heavily modified in the 19th century) seems similar to the Crickhowell Bridge, it's very different in that there's only one sidewalk on the east side of the bridge and it's very narrow. Also, if you've approached from the canal you're probably on the wrong side of Merthyr Road and it's difficult to cross the busy street to get to the sidewalk.

Access to the Crickhowell Bridge was regulated with traffic lights that enforced alternate one-way traffic across that bridge, but no such scheme is in place here. The trick is to follow the roundabout just north of the Waitrose in counter-clockwise fashion. This way you cross Merthyr Road with the benefit of a crosswalk and pedestrian island.

Even with the sidewalk it's still unnerving to cross the bridge, but thankfully the Monmouthshire County Council has approved building a pedestrian and bicycle bridge adjacent to the road bridge.

If your goal is to visit the castle, you'll want to step down to the path through Castle Meadows just after you cross the bridge, then follow the path next to the Usk until turning north to the castle. Altogether it's a 1.6mi/2.57km walk or ride from Tod's Bridge. Luckily cyclists can ride on the path through Castle Meadows because it's actually part of NCR 46.

Abergavenny is a great walking town, which is good because you'll be doing a lot of it. There are several pedestrian friendly streets including Nevill, St. John's and Market streets. Cross Street also becomes the car free High Street.

## Attractions

**Abergavenny Castle** Ⓦ is the largest and most complete castle convenient to the canal that you'll encounter. The castle, which dates back to just after the Norman Conquest, is still a ruin, but it retains  a large stretch of curtain wall, much of the gatehouse and a tower. However the castle appears much grander thanks to a Victorian hunting lodge that now serves as Abergavenny Museum. The museum is open everyday except Wednesday from 11am–4pm.

The castle is also improved by

Castle Meadows, a floodplain crisscrossed by paths, which makes for a pleasant walk along the Usk. **Linda Vista Gardens** Ⓦ also sits above the meadows and is just one of the many parks that helped Abergavenny win a Green Flag Award in 2017.

You'll also find **St. Mary's Priory Church** Ⓦ just north of the castle. Originally a Benedictine monastery, it survived Henry VIII's Reformation to become the parish church. The church, which dates back to the 1100s, stands on Roman ruins and is known for its monumental tombs and effigies, including the Tree of Jesse, a carved oak figure depicting the lineage of Christ. Although the surviving more than life-size figure is impressive, it would originally have shown a carved tree growing upwards perhaps 25 feet. The tombs, effigies, the church's ten bells and adjacent tithe barn (which houses the **Abergavenny Tourist Informa-**

 The charm of Wharfingers Cottage masks the canal's tight turn. It's not too bad going south, but heading north requires the use of poles to avoid ramming the bank of the winding hole.

tion & National Park Centre ) contribute to St. Mary's Priory Church being called the "Westminster Abbey of Wales."

## Lodging

Originally a Georgian coaching inn, the 31-room **Angel Hotel** at the corner of Cross and Lower Castle streets is the most impressive lodging in Abergavenny. Services include a car park and one accessible room. The hotel also has several nearby cottages, the adjacent Angel Bakery and sister property **The Abergavenny Hotel**. The locally owned Angel also offers a posh afternoon and high tea (which is a fine complement to the cozier **Emmeline's Tea Room** at the corner of Baker Street and Lewis's Lane). The Oak Room and Foxhunter's Bar are also found at The Angel Hotel.

**The King's Head** is on the other side of Cross Street from The Angel. It dates from the late 16th-century, is also a former coaching inn, and is family owned. On-site parking is available with a surcharge. Regency 59 is the hotel's restaurant.

**The King's Arms**, which can be found at Nevill and Castle streets, is—*surprise*—a late 16th-century former coaching inn. Like the other hotels mentioned, room rates include a free breakfast. The distinctive yellow hotel has free parking except on Tuesday market days. Selected dog friendly rooms are available at a £15 surcharge.

The **Bridge Inn** and **Premier Inn**  are the most convenient to the canal. The four-room, pet friendly Bridge Inn sits next to the busy Merthyr Road over the bridge. Supposedly there's free parking but I'm puzzled as to its location. A beer garden overlooks the Usk. Premier Inn is a standard chain hotel beside the A465.

**The Great Western Abergavenny** (not shown on the map) is an en suite B&B as well as home to Black Sheep Backpackers, which has some great rates for groups, with dorm rooms for up to 10 people. The Great Western was a Victorian railway hotel and is next to the train station.

There are too many B&Bs and guest houses to describe separately, but an interesting self-catered apartment choice can be found at **The Old Police Station**. The apartments are named after Sherlock Holmes characters (the police station is on Baker Street), although the modern rooms don't reflect the Great Detective's Victorian era.

Beacon Park Boats *(see page 27)* offers three cottages at Llanfoist Wharf: Dry Dock Cottage with a window that sits at water level, Incline Cottage and Wharfinger's Cottage (the white cottage sleeps six). The large building with a crane is a private residence.

## Pubs and restaurants

There are too many to list individually but several stand out. The highest concentration of restaurants is on Cross Street, which then becomes the High Street. You'll find the second location of the Gurkha Corner restaurant (the other being in Brecon), serving Himalayan fare *(see page 44)*. It's just off the High Street in the interesting triangle

*If you walk to Abergavenny from Tod's Bridge on the canal, you'll pass by the very pretty Saint Faiths Parish Church Llanfoist*

formed by Nevill Street and the High Street.

**The Coliseum** Ⓦ is interesting because this Wetherspoon pub is in the old Coliseum Cinema (the nearby Baker Street Cinema can still supply your need to view the latest Marvel film). **The Balti Delight** Ⓦ calls to me because I'm quite fond of this Indian/Pakistani hybrid dish born in Birmingham. The 800-pound gorilla in the room Angel Hotel also offers lots of dining/drinking choices.

Another unique space is **The Art Shop & Chapel** Ⓦ, actually two spaces about two minutes apart. The chapel (behind Abergavenny Market) has the kitchen and special events such as guest authors and musicians while the art shop has the gallery as well as art supplies.

## Shopping

As with most of the towns and villages along the canal, most Abergavenny shops are local, but there are some nationally branded stores north of Abergavenny Market Hall next to Frogmore Street. The **Cibi Walk Shopping Arcade** Ⓦ, where you can find a **Poundland** Ⓦ (the UK equivalent of a dollar store) and **WH Smith** Ⓦ as well as local shops, runs from Frogmore to King Street. On King Street you can find an outlet of the **Argos** Ⓦ catalog/online shopping store. You'll also find an outlet of **Mountain Warehouse** Ⓦ on the High Street.

## Groceries

There are plenty of grocery stores in the area and the most convenient to the canal is the **Waitrose** Ⓦ south of the Usk and just before the bridge of death … err, Abergavenny Bridge. You'll also find a **Morrisons**, **ALDI** and small **Tescos** Ⓦ. The Morrisons, incidentally, is built on the site of the Abergavenny Cattle Market, which died in 2013.

The best place to buy groceries, at least on Tuesday, Friday and Saturday, is the **Abergavenny Market** Ⓦ. It's not hard to find because its Victorian clock tower stands higher than anything else on the High Street. You'll also find public toilets in the Brewery Yard behind the market.

## Festivals

The market is also the epicenter of the **Abergavenny Food Festival** Ⓦ (held in September), although food festival locations can be found throughout the town, even on the castle grounds. The festival attracts top name chefs and more than 30,000 visitors so book lodging early if you plan to visit Abergavenny during the two-day event.

Other festivals include the **Steam Rally** Ⓦ in May (held in Bailey Park), the **Festival of Cycling** Ⓦ in June, the **Writing Festival** Ⓦ in April, the Music Festival (oddly there's no permanent website) in May and the **Arts Festival** Ⓦ in June.

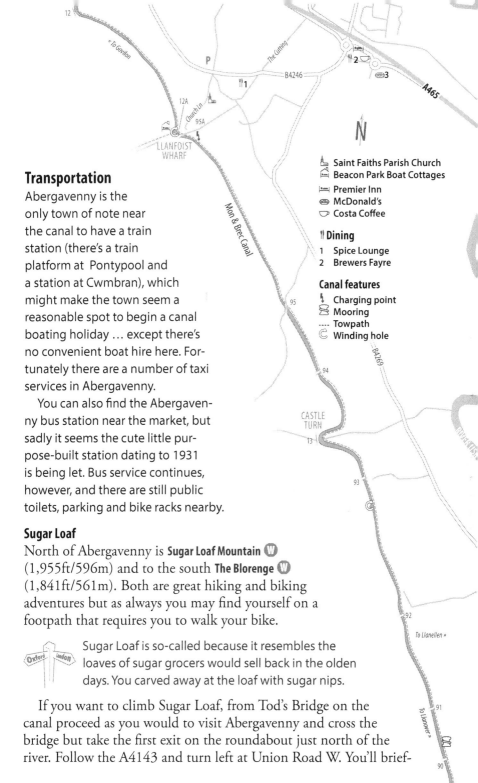

## Transportation

Abergavenny is the only town of note near the canal to have a train station (there's a train platform at Pontypool and a station at Cwmbran), which might make the town seem a reasonable spot to begin a canal boating holiday … except there's no convenient boat hire here. Fortunately there are a number of taxi services in Abergavenny.

You can also find the Abergavenny bus station near the market, but sadly it seems the cute little purpose-built station dating to 1931 is being let. Bus service continues, however, and there are still public toilets, parking and bike racks nearby.

## Sugar Loaf

North of Abergavenny is **Sugar Loaf Mountain** Ⓦ (1,955ft/596m) and to the south **The Blorenge** Ⓦ (1,841ft/561m). Both are great hiking and biking adventures but as always you may find yourself on a footpath that requires you to walk your bike.

Sugar Loaf is so-called because it resembles the loaves of sugar grocers would sell back in the olden days. You carved away at the loaf with sugar nips.

If you want to climb Sugar Loaf, from Tod's Bridge on the canal proceed as you would to visit Abergavenny and cross the bridge but take the first exit on the roundabout just north of the river. Follow the A4143 and turn left at Union Road W. You'll brief-

Saint Faiths Parish Church
Beacon Park Boat Cottages
Premier Inn
McDonald's
Costa Coffee

**Dining**
1   Spice Lounge
2   Brewers Fayre

**Canal features**
Charging point
Mooring
Towpath
Winding hole

ly join the A40 heading west (away from Abergavenny) and turn north on an unnamed road that will connect to Cresta Road. Cresta Road travels north until it intersects Pentre Road. Turn left and then a quick right (north) to another unnamed road. You'll repeat this process when the unnamed road meets Pentre Lane. Turn left again and this unnamed road continues north until it begins circling Sugar Loaf to the west. You'll find a National Trust parking lot and yet another unnamed and unpaved "road" that leads to the summit of Sugar Loaf.

 I couldn't quite shoehorn a map to Sugar Loaf in this book, but you can find my **Google map** Ⓦ showing routes to Sugar Loaf, The Blorenge and Llanfoist Incline.

This route is suitable for hiking and biking. Cyclists can either ride in traffic or use the pavement until Cresta Road meets Pentre Road. The unnamed road after this is a single lane but there are frequent cutouts to allow cars to pass. This is a 5mi/8.1km route with 1,933ft/589m of elevation change and you can retrace your steps to return, but a **National Trust map** Ⓦ shows a loop that continues down the east flank of Sugar Loaf.

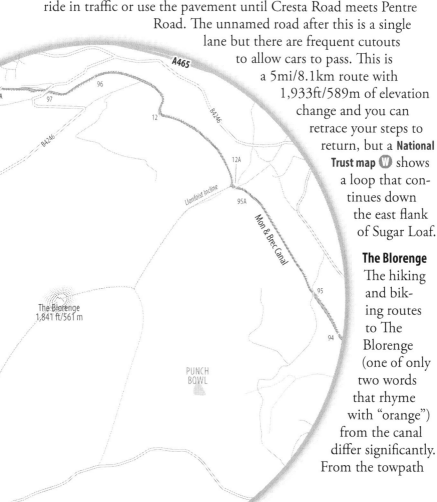

### The Blorenge

The hiking and biking routes to The Blorenge (one of only two words that rhyme with "orange") from the canal differ significantly. From the towpath

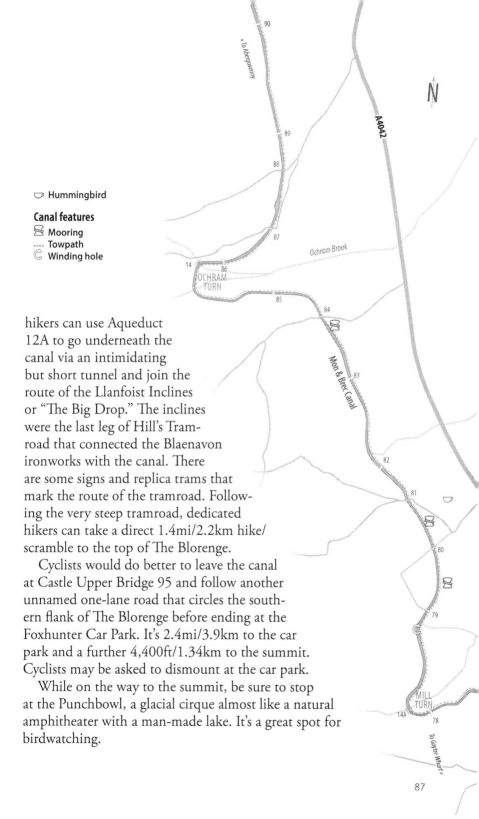

N

90

89

88

87

86

85

84

83

82

81

80

79

78

14

OCHRAM TURN

A4042

To Abergavenny

Ochram Brook

Mon & Brec Canal

MILL TURN

14A

To Goytre Wharf

🐦 Hummingbird

**Canal features**
🛏 Mooring
---- Towpath
🌀 Winding hole

hikers can use Aqueduct 12A to go underneath the canal via an intimidating but short tunnel and join the route of the Llanfoist Inclines or "The Big Drop." The inclines were the last leg of Hill's Tramroad that connected the Blaenavon ironworks with the canal. There are some signs and replica trams that mark the route of the tramroad. Following the very steep tramroad, dedicated hikers can take a direct 1.4mi/2.2km hike/scramble to the top of The Blorenge.

Cyclists would do better to leave the canal at Castle Upper Bridge 95 and follow another unnamed one-lane road that circles the southern flank of The Blorenge before ending at the Foxhunter Car Park. It's 2.4mi/3.9km to the car park and a further 4,400ft/1.34km to the summit. Cyclists may be asked to dismount at the car park.

While on the way to the summit, be sure to stop at the Punchbowl, a glacial cirque almost like a natural amphitheater with a man-made lake. It's a great spot for birdwatching.

87

You'll see many references to Foxhunter in the area. The show jumping horse won the only Gold Medal for Great Britain in the 1952 Summer Olympics and is buried on The Blorenge.

## Llanellen and Llanover

After Abergavenny the canal hugs the eastern border of Brecon Beacons National Park and just manages to remain in the park until Pontypool. By the village of Llanellen, of which there is little to report apart from it often winning the Best Kept Small Village award, the Usk and the canal part company, the canal heading south and the river east.

The countryside around the canal greatly changes after Abergavenny. After leaving the bulk of The Blorenge behind the canal no longer clings so tightly to the hill sides and to the east the Usk Valley is broad and flat. The canal becomes very quiet and of little moment. You'll pass by Llanellen and Llanover without notice and until Goytre Wharf time will pass by uneventfully.

You may also regret if you forgot to buy groceries in Abergavenny because there are no pubs, restaurants or stores apart from the **Hummingbird** ☕ coffee shop in Llanover, a 960ft/293m walk from the canal.

The canal makes a very tight hairpin curve (Castle Turn) about midway between Llanfoist and Llanellen that's guaranteed to cause a boat to run aground and then another tight turn (Ochram Turn) between Llanellen and Llanover. Castle Turn takes place with the canal quite overgrown with trees adding to a sense of doom if you're stuck. There were some picnic tables here with CRT volunteers taking a break from their chores and they helped us get unstuck. And there's another tight turn after Llanover (Mill Turn).

One item of interest here is **Llanover House** ☕, built in 1837 and the home of Augusta Waddington, Lady Llanover. She was a proponent of all things Welsh and her husband, Benjamin Hall, may be the "Ben" for whom the Westminster bell "Big Ben" is named. The substantial gardens and the house are open to visitors selected days each summer.

I have to confess this part of the canal was something of a trial for me. I view the success of a canal trip in how many museums I've visited, how many historic markers I've read and how many miles traveled. But there is very little to do but relax and take in the scenery. This part of the canal is a good opportunity to take a shower, cook a meal or sort through your luggage—all at the risk of missing some tiny moment like seeing wildlife or the sun dancing on the water.

## Information

Visit Abergavenny
bit.ly/2Fq6hB0

Abergavenny Cycle Group
bit.ly/2OdQQ1u

Abergavenny Now
bit.ly/2Tnz7Wh

Abergavenny Local History Society
bit.ly/2TYnFoB

Abergavenny walk/cycle maps
bit.ly/2JNLbk6

National Trust Sugar Loaf map
bit.ly/2X8Kesm

Abergavenny Tourist Info&Nat'l Pk Centre
bit.ly/2Y6GaG3

## Attractions

Abergavenny Castle & Museum
bit.ly/2HDOx7I

St. Mary's Priory Church
bit.ly/2FsX9dP

Linda Vista Gardens
bit.ly/2TUaplI

Sugar Loaf Mountain
bit.ly/2YZsHPY

The Blorenge
bit.ly/2MPcsTo

Llanover House
bit.ly/2JfoS4G

## Festivals

Abergavenny Food Festival
bit.ly/2Wh42FI

Abergavenny Steam Rally
bit.ly/2OpufiG

Abergavenny Festival of Cycling
bit.ly/2TY9uk0

Abergavenny Writing Festival
bit.ly/2UXWAiA

Abergavenny Arts Festival
bit.ly/2HSsjOq

## Transportation

Fast Cars of Abergavenny Taxi
bit.ly/2TsZytW

Julian's Taxis
bit.ly/2UX2Rv4

Lewis Taxis
bit.ly/2WmeTyg

Terry's Taxi
1873 854678

Train 2 Taxi
bit.ly/2Os5v9n

Abergavenny Bus Station
bit.ly/2YKaMxV

Abergavenny Train Station
bit.ly/2TNiVhu

## Hotels

The Abergavenny Hotel
bit.ly/2UslM3z

The Angel Hotel
bit.ly/2FVkztO

The
Black Lion
bit.ly/2WGkH5L

The Bridge
Inn
bit.ly/2WFUpRa

Kings Arms
Hotel
bit.ly/2uKYB6a

The Kings
Head
bit.ly/2WI2Yeb

Premier Inn
bit.ly/31x89QA

The Great Western
Abergavenny
bit.ly/2O226Sr

## B&Bs

Blorenge View Bed
& Breakfast
bit.ly/2WZpXpR

Castle Cottage at
the Angel
bit.ly/2Fp28Nk

The Old
Police Station
bit.ly/2RtE7tk

Ryvington
House
bit.ly/2ZEMhSi

Trelough
House
bit.ly/2N4T6eD

## Dining

The Art Shop
and Chapel
bit.ly/2FVMFoA

Auberge
Abergavenny
bit.ly/2OIlaBP

The
Bayleaf
bit.ly/2YJwSk8

Boonta Too
Thai Restaurant
bit.ly/2WLkGxI

Cinnamon
Tree
bit.ly/2HUT5Xt

Coach &
Horses
bit.ly/2KdwUxk

The
Coliseum
bit.ly/2I9PdRF

The Foxhunter
Bar
bit.ly/2Vh4e7N

The
Greyhound Vaults
bit.ly/2FVoNSa

The Grofield
Inn
bit.ly/2UwzFOg

The Gurkha
Corner
bit.ly/2Uekc6f

Hens &
Chickens
bit.ly/2Uud70L

Kong's
Oriental
bit.ly/2J4VXQE

Luigi's
Café
bit.ly/2CRfQr2

The Oak
Room
bit.ly/2WKqt6i

Railway
Inn
bit.ly/2HVqS2v

Somerset
Arms
bit.ly/2WLpxi3

Regency 59
bit.ly/2WLpxi3

Station
Hotel
bit.ly/2OKmmof

Sundarbon
Kitchen
bit.ly/2YPWBrp

Tamarind
Restaurant & Bar
bit.ly/2HTB7Ew

Y Cantreff
Inn
bit.ly/33EgIeu

## Cafés, bakeries, tea rooms

*Abergavenny*

 The Angel
Bakery
bit.ly/2Y7wD1C

 Caffè
Nero
bit.ly/2xi79D7

 Coffee #1
Abergavenny
bit.ly/2J0aD2i

 Costa
Coffee
bit.ly/2RstfM7

 Cwtch
Cafe
bit.ly/2N2PyJY

 Fig Tree
Espresso
bit.ly/2L5EqcI

 Greggs
bit.ly/2Y3HWrz

 Harry's Sandwich
and Coffee Bar
bit.ly/2FmfGZW

 The
Little Treat
bit.ly/2Ky9ylp

 Oasis
Snack Bar
bit.ly/2J42ied

 Parsons
Bakery
bit.ly/2Xs1bxU

 Play Den Coffee
Shop
bit.ly/2x5Oqdx

 Afternoon Tea at
the Angel
bit.ly/2x67rg2

 Emmeline's Tea
Room
bit.ly/2N2c0Tu

*Llanellen*

 Hummingbird
bit.ly/2FsaaFa

## Chemists

 Boots
bit.ly/2Kuzbnh

 Lloyd's
Pharmacy
bit.ly/2N3u9Aq

 H Shackleton
bit.ly/2N3EkFb

## Fast food

 Codfather
bit.ly/2L0MKdI

 Market Street
Fish Shop
bit.ly/2ZBSTRt

 Abergavenny Kebab
House
bit.ly/2WXhhv4

 Balti
Delight
bit.ly/2WYOThg

 Dominos
bit.ly/2ZxtMzo

 Pick
a Pizza
bit.ly/2WZdFc2

 Marmaris Kebab
and Pizza
bit.ly/2XLhu9h

 Sing Lee
bit.ly/2x9ONns

 Town
Gate
bit.ly/2KuVJEr

## Groceries

 Abergavenny
Market
bit.ly/2LE0oUa

 ALDI
bit.ly/2N3iQs0

 Morrisons
bit.ly/2Ruu47u

 Tesco
Metro
bit.ly/2Fqip4D

## The Monmouthshire & Brecon Canal

 Waitrose
bit.ly/2Fpfycj

 WH Smith
bit.ly/2YGOTDl

 Gateway
Cycles
bit.ly/2XriT4Q

### Shopping

 Argos
Abergavenny
bit.ly/2IvC6d3

 Savers Health &
Beauty
bit.ly/2LwVacZ

 Nevill Hall
Hospital
bit.ly/2WWSEyX

### Miscellaneous

 Cibi Walk
Shopping Arcade
bit.ly/2YZjbN1

 Baker Street
Cinema
bit.ly/2N53vHr

 Mountain
Warehouse
bit.ly/2ZJKz2l

 Abergavenny
Post Office
bit.ly/2KyjDyM

 Poundland
bit.ly/2ISZUXi

 Borough
Theatre
bit.ly/31QDQFJ

You'll find nice views of the Black Mountains from the canal as it heads south from Abergavenny. Here we're looking roughly north at The Skirrid or Ysgyryd Fawr (1594ft/486m). Notice also the fishing platforms meant for wheelchair access to the canal.

*These informative signs are found all along the canal. The drawings are from the book 200 years of The Monmouthshire and the Brecknock & Abergavenny Canals. This sign shows the lime kilns at Goytre Wharf, which you can see in the distance.*

# Goytre Wharf to Five Locks (and beyond)
(7.31mi/11.76km)[1]

The sight of Goytre Wharf comes as a welcome interruption, especially for hikers and cyclists. You'll find a CRT Visitor's Centre here, a café in the summer months, restrooms and the well-preserved lime kilns. After many canal trips I'm something of a lime kiln snob, but I have to admit the Goytre kilns are in good nick. The kilns have been restored and they actually give a good idea of how the kilns were used, loading limestone and coal from the top and removing the lime from the bottom.

You'll also find Red Line Boats *(see page 27)* here where besides hiring a narrowboat you can rent bikes and canoes. There's also a marina and chandlery. Red Line Boats also lets out the Aqueduct Cottage, which back in the day was the weighbridge for carts loading and unloading narrowboats.

 You can also at Goytre Wharf buy one-day fishing permits for the canal between bridges 77 and 73, but you must also have an **Environment Agency rod license** Ⓦ. There are a number of wheelchair accessible fishing platforms along the canal.

---

1   Distance shown is from Goytre Wharf to the end of CRT control of the canal just south of Solomon's Bridge. It's an extra 0.77mi/1.24km to Five Locks Road.

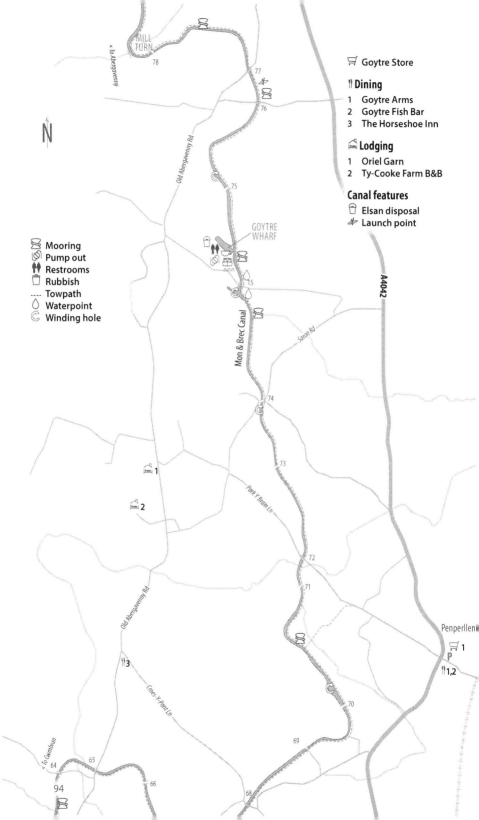

**N**

MILL
TURN

« To Abergavenny

78

77

76

Old Abergavenny Rd

75

GOYTRE
WHARF

15

Mon & Brec Canal

Saron Rd

74

73

Park Y Brain Ln

72

71

Old Abergavenny Rd

70

69

Coes-y-Pant Ln

« To Gwmbran

64    65

66

94

68

A4042

Penperllen

1

P

1,2

☐ Goytre Store

**🍴 Dining**
1   Goytre Arms
2   Goytre Fish Bar
3   The Horseshoe Inn

**🏠 Lodging**
1   Oriel Garn
2   Ty-Cooke Farm B&B

**Canal features**
☐ Elsan disposal
⚓ Launch point

☐ Mooring
☐ Pump out
♛ Restrooms
☐ Rubbish
---- Towpath
◊ Waterpoint
☾ Winding hole

1

2

3

*The scenery after Goytre Wharf is stunning and well worth the effort to explore. You can see the towpath above with the canal to the right (outside the picture).*

Unfortunately one of the nice attractions of the wharf will require a few years to re-establish. Many visitors have remarked on enjoying a walk in the woods north of Goytre Wharf but those woods were recently harvested, leaving a pretty barren patch of ground. There are, however, many trails in the area that you can find on an Ordnance Survey map and just south of the wharf you'll find a pleasant little path through some woods that leads to Penperlleni. This will come in handy, especially if you arrive at Goytre Wharf in the off months (we were there the second week of September). We found the café and canal center closed so we walked to the Goytre Arms in Penperlleni. In mere seconds the footpath makes you think you're in a vast forest before suddenly dropping you onto Parc Y Brain Lane. It's a short walk on the one-lane road to the intersection with the A4042.

Less pleasant is the fact **The Goytre Arms** and the **Goytre Fish Bar & Tandoori** Ⓦ takeaway is on the other side of the very busy A4042. The road curves on either side of the intersection hiding oncoming traffic from view. Your only strategy is to take a deep breath, pray to whatever canal god you hold dear and run like hell. The Goytre Arms, however, is well worth the effort, or if you want something to take back to the boat try the fish bar. There's also a recently opened convenience store

# The Monmouthshire & Brecon Canal

N

63

67 68

To Goytre Wharf
Chwyd-Y-Clap Ln

Pentre Ln

Mamhilad

62  ‖ 1

Old Abergavenny Rd

Foily Ln

Old Cobbled Rd

61

60

Usk Rd

1

59

58

A4042

Folly Ln

57

Mon & Brec Canal

56

‖ 2

2

PONTYPOOL
PARK

55  2

Usk Rd

To Cwmbran

96

53

## ‖ Dining
1   The Star inn
2   The Horse & Jockey

## ▣ Attractions
1   Pontypool Folly
2   Arbour, Shell Grotto

## Canal features
☒ Mooring
···· Towpath
Ⓒ Winding hole

if you need milk, soft drinks or something stronger to replenish your boat's supplies.

A local farmer also recommended **The Horseshoe Inn** and **The Star Inn** 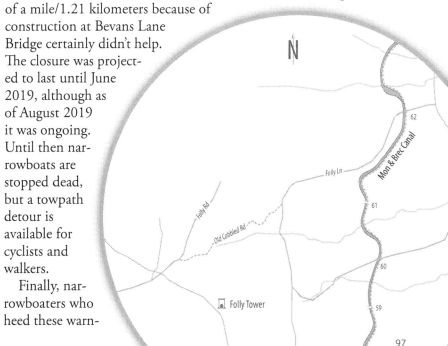 but those were too far from our mooring between bridges 71 and 70. Bridges 69 or 68 are more convenient to travel to The Horseshoe Inn on Old Abergavenny Road, or Bridge 62 for The Star Inn. You'll also find two lodging options on Old Abergavenny Road, **Oriel Garn** self-catered cottage and **Ty-Cooke Farm B&B** . Just north of Bridge 70 is a winding hole if you want to turn around and avoid the final stretch of the canal.

## The end of the canal

There's an unmistakable melancholy for those who travel the last stretch of the Mon & Brec. Few boaters go south of Goytre Wharf and fewer still go south of Pontymoile Basin, and the blame for this reluctance can be spread wide. Narrowboat hire companies understandably warn their customers of the weeds that increasingly choke the canal south of Goytre Wharf. A narrowboat vacation isn't as enjoyable if you're constantly opening the weed hatch and clearing the propeller.

The Canal & River Trust and other volunteer groups possibly could do more to mitigate the weeds, but I'm well aware resources are stretched thin. And the 2018 closure of the final three-quarters of a mile/1.21 kilometers because of construction at Bevans Lane Bridge certainly didn't help. The closure was projected to last until June 2019, although as of August 2019 it was ongoing. Until then narrowboats are stopped dead, but a towpath detour is available for cyclists and walkers.

Finally, narrowboaters who heed these warnings are also the problem. On our 2018 trip we stopped our boat just south of Goytre Wharf and I cycled the remaining seven miles to Five Locks Road, the end of the canal. By bridge 58 I saw increasing signs of weeds and by Pontymoile Basin the canal looked like it was covered by a green blanket.[2] South of the closure at bridge 47 the weeds were standing above the water.

 The winding hole north of Solomon's Bridge 47 can handle boats up to 45 feet long. At 55 feet our boat would have been too long. Larger boats should turn around at Pontymoile Basin. The winding hole at Five Locks Basin can accommodate boats up to 60 feet … if you can get there.

Nevertheless we talked to people who *had* taken their narrowboats to Pontymoile Basin and they gave *African Queen*-like accounts of clearing the propeller and running aground, but there was a discernible pride in the accomplishment.

So really everyone is to blame and *no one is to blame* for the state of the canal south of Goytre Wharf. If people avoid this last stretch because of a reputation for weeds, the weed problem will just get worse. And this is a real shame because this part of the canal is quite pretty. From Bridge 71 to Usk Road Bridge 55 you'll see nothing but the occasional farm or cottage … and beautiful countryside.

## Pontypool

One attraction somewhat far from the canal is the **Pontypool Folly** ⓦ, originally an 18th-century tower that was demolished at the start of World War II to deny German bombers an easy landmark. It was rebuilt and reopened in 1994. Cyclists should leave the canal at Bridge 62 and ride west on Folly Lane and then take the "Old Cobbled Road" west when Folly Lane turns south. This 0.35mi/0.56km "road" is really a footpath that connects to Folly Road. The folly is actually on a working farm so you'll leave the road and walk south east to the tower.

 You should either plan to use a mountain bike on the "Old Cobbled Road" (0.35mi/0.57km) or walk your bike as the road is steep and rough. Locals claim it's an old Roman road and it's possible the Romans were the last to maintain it. Of course you can just ride the path up from Usk Road described below.

2   In August 2019 the Torfaen Council introduced 2mm weevils (small beetles) to a section of the canal near Ty Coch with the hope the insects would eat the water fern

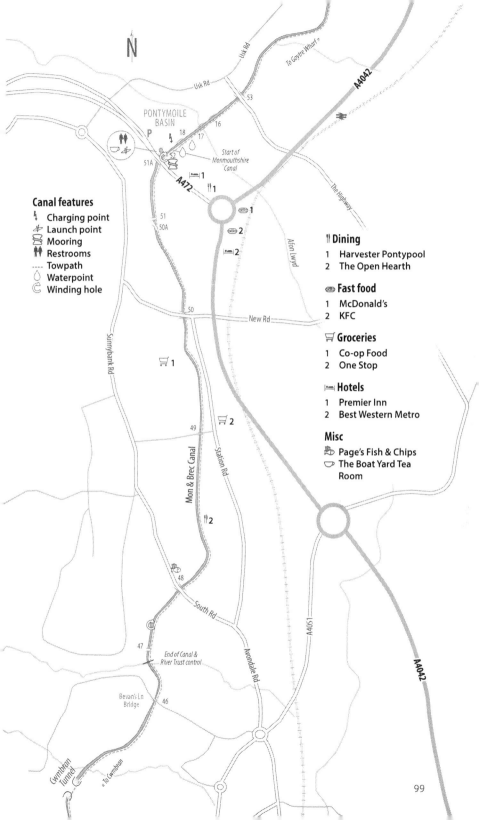

N

PONTYMOILE BASIN

Usk Rd

To Goytre Wharf

A4042

Usk Rd

53

16

P 18

17

Start of
Monmouthshire
Canal

51A

A472 1

1

The Highway

51

50A

1

2

Afon Lwyd

2

## Canal features
- **↟** Charging point
- **⚓** Launch point
- **⧈** Mooring
- **👫** Restrooms
- **┄┄** Towpath
- **◊** Waterpoint
- **℃** Winding hole

## 🍴 Dining
1. Harvester Pontypool
2. The Open Hearth

## 🍔 Fast food
1. McDonald's
2. KFC

## 🛒 Groceries
1. Co-op Food
2. One Stop

## 🛏 Hotels
1. Premier Inn
2. Best Western Metro

## Misc
- 🐟 Page's Fish & Chips
- ☕ The Boat Yard Tea Room

50

New Rd

Sunnybank Rd

1

2

49

Mon & Brec Canal

Station Rd

2

48

South Rd

A4051

47

End of Canal &
River Trust control

Avondale Rd

A4042

Bevan's Ln
Bridge

46

Cwmbran
Tunnel

To Cwmbran

99

The footpath continues and eventually meets Folly Lane and allows you to make a big loop back to Bridge 62, or you can continue south and visit the grotto in **Pontypool Park** . The Shell Grotto (or Hermitage) was built by John Hanbury, who also built the folly. It's a good climb up to the grotto, however. Unfortunately one complication of visiting these attractions is that you're not allowed to cycle through the park but if you stick to something that looks like a road you "should" be OK.

 Some rich landowners even employed hermits to live in caves and it's a popular myth a hermit built and then lived in the Shell Grotto.

For a more direct route, cyclists and hikers can leave the canal as shown on my **online map**  at Pontymoile Basin and enter the park through some grand gates on Usk Road. Lock your bike and then walk 1,800ft/549m northeast on a footpath to the grotto and the arbor.

## A pleasant ride

On my ride south of Goytre Wharf I rose early and saw the sun rise over pastures dotted with picturesque cows. It was an easy bike ride, but as I wore shorts my legs were shredded by vegetation that occasionally crowded the towpath. I never even noticed this, however, entranced as I was by taking photos of horses, stopping to eat blackberries (this was early September) and marveling at the golden light.

After Usk Road, you'll pass houses on the non-towpath side of the canal, and on the towpath side you'll pass Panteg Cemetery, however trees will prevent you from seeing much on either side. As you continue south you'll see boats in private moorings as you approach Pontymoile Basin. You'll pass over three aqueducts as you approach the basin but you'll probably only notice the one over the Afon Lwyd.

 The original Monmouthshire Canal met the Brecknock & Abergavenny Canal at **Pontymoile Basin** . You'll notice the canal narrows as it approaches Bridge 52 because there was a stop lock separating the two canals. A lockkeeper who lived at the distinctive white Junction Cottage would gauge boats here and assess a toll. Today the cottage is used as the residence of the basin and marina caretakers. The basin also marked the start of the Pontnewynydd arm of the Monmouthshire Canal, but the canal and the railway that replaced it are buried under the A472.

The basin is a great place to relax after a bike ride. You'll find a car park, restrooms, waterpoint and toilets here, as well as the Boat Yard

*The sight of the canal disappearing into a culvert just before Five Locks Road is dispiriting. It does reappear on the south side of the road, but at the moment the diversion effectively closes the canal to navigation.*

Tea Room, which is a permanently beached old narrowboat. The tea room is open almost year round, but with reduced hours in the winter months. And as mentioned earlier, the winding hole next to Bridge 52 is the last turning place for most boats headed south until the Bevans Lane construction is finished.

A notable feature just south of the basin are two bridges that cross the canal, first a railway viaduct that crosses the canal diagonally (a skew bridge) and then Bridge 51, which crosses the canal at a right angle and then passes through an arch of the viaduct. (Cyclists and hikers intent on following the canal should avoid this bridge.) So we have a viaduct over a bridge over a canal. The railway, however, is abandoned and the bridge is probably forgotten to all except those on the canal.

 The rail line was part of the Pontypool, Caerleon and Newport Railway that was actually part of the Monmouthshire Railway and Canal Company (later gobbled up by the Great Western Railway). The rail line ran next to what is now County "Panteg" Hospital. The hospital was originally a Victorian workhouse. A small rail line to carry coal to the workhouse/hospital also crossed the canal here and you can try to spot remnants of that viaduct.

After the basin the canal will do its best to continue shielding your view but at Bridge 50 you'll clearly see the back side of houses on the towpath side. I enjoy urban canals as much as rural ones so I found this stretch very enjoyable, although I did have to cross a street and

## The Monmouthshire & Brecon Canal

### 🍴 Dining
1  The Old Bridgend Inn
2  The Waterloo

### 🛒 Groceries
1  ALDI
2  Sainsbury's
3  Lidl
4  Asda

### 🏨 Hotels
1  Premier Inn
2  Best Western Metro

### 🍟 Fish and chips
1  Pontnewydd Fish Bar
2  Page's Fish & Chips

### Misc
🍟 Page's Fish & Chips
☕ The Lock Cafe
✚ Lloyds Pharmacy

### 🚗 Car hire
1  Avondale Vehicle Hire
2  Enterprise Rent-a-Car

**Canal features**
⚓ Lock
  Removed / non-
  functioning lock
---- Towpath

negotiate some gates at Bridges 49 and 48.

Between those bridges, however, you'll find the very well regarded **The Open Hearth** 🍺. It's family run, dog friendly and has a cozy atmosphere. The Panteg Cricket Club pitch is just opposite the pub on the off side of the canal. Further south is The Crown Inn but it's listed as permanently closed. The nearby **Page's Fish & Chips** 🍺, however, is still a going concern.

There's very little left of the navigable canal at this point.

CRT control of the canal ends at Bridge 47 and the remaining 0.8mi/1.26km is under the control of the Torfaen County Borough Council. The work at Bevan's Lane Bridge, however, denies most of that to boaters.

One feature of interest on this last stretch is the very short (perhaps 76yd/70m) Cwmbran Tunnel. It was still navigable before the Bevans Lane construction but I assume few boats have braved the tunnel in recent memory. The towpath continues above ground giving cyclists a little bit of a climb.

## The end of the line ... for now

At Five Locks Road, the canal disappears in a culvert and reappears on the other side of the road. South of Five Locks Road you can find a rusted sign proclaiming the Five Locks Restoration Scheme, which was sadly over optimistic. There seems to be some movement toward restoring the rest of the original Monmouthshire Canal, but it still seems a herculean task.

Seen on anything other than a bright sunny day, the remains of the five locks are quite depressing. It's hard to realize this must have been a hive of activity when laden narrowboats negotiated the locks. Concrete structures mimic where the canal gates would have stood (the "gates" have openings to allow water to flow) and you can still see the side ponds that supplied the locks with sufficient water. It's almost pretty if you can avoid sight of submerged shopping trolleys and other trash or after a cleanup by volunteer groups.

The towpath, however, remains in good shape (although you do have to cross Five Locks Road) and it continues south for another 5.45mi/8.76km. You might think this stretch of canal only for those who obsessively complete things, but cyclists or walkers who travel the towpath will be rewarded with the restoration efforts on the **Ty Coch Lock Flight** 🕐. Various groups including the Monmouthshire, Brecon & Abergavenny Canal Trust, Torfaen County Borough Council and Inland

Waterways Association have restored six of the seven locks of the flight using innovative modular metal gates. Wooden gates must be replaced every 25 years, but the metal gates can last a hundred years or more, require less maintenance and can be installed by volunteers without heavy equipment.

Unfortunately despite this restoration the canal is quite unnavigable after Five Locks Road as it often flows under roadways through a culvert and disappears completely for long stretches. Fortunately the towpath, which is also National Cycle Route 49, continues uninterrupted except for street-level crossings. And despite being a built-up area with superstores, restaurants and fast food outlets, the canal remains relatively quiet. Most of the congestion begins about Mount Pleasant Road/Commercial Street and disappears about Hollybush Way and the Ty Coch flight. In fact the canal/cycle route through Malpas is serene. Along the way you'll pass a number of canal bridges and derelict locks, many with surviving lock gates. It's picturesque in a tumbled down days of past glory kind of way and not in a "Is that a mattress down there?" way. The canal remains watered although choked with weeds in many places and the towpath is a little rutted but it's still a body of water winding through the countryside. This bit gives reason to hope the canal could be navigable again all the way to Newport and the Usk.

 Full disclosure: I have not traveled much south of Five Locks Road so this information is based on following the Monmouthshire Canal and the Crumlin Arm via Google, OpenStreetMap and Ordnance Survey maps, reading news stories about restoration efforts, watching videos and scouring canal guides.

## The Usk and Newport Docks

The canal essentially ends at that roundabout where the M4 crosses the A4051.[3] Fortunately hikers and cyclists can continue the journey to what was the southern terminus of the canal by following a succession of National Cycle Routes. From Abergavenny south, NCR 49 uses the towpath of the Mon & Brec Canal until passing under the M4 and ending in a "T" with NCR 47. NCR 47 then follows Crindau Pill, which is a flood defense diversion that flows into the Usk. However instead of going all the way to the Usk, NCR 47 ends in a "T" with NCR 88 (traveling north-south). This cycleway roughly follows the path of the Usk.

---

3    This is also where the Crumlin Arm of the Monmouthshire Canal begins

The route I'm suggesting is more or less the original path of the Monmouthshire Canal to the Newport Docks. The canal actually predates the docks and connected to the Usk at a basin near Llanarth Street. Almost nothing is left of the canal other than the Crindau Pill. I realize these directions are quite complicated so I've created a **Google Map** Ⓦ of this route.

NCR 88 continues south roughly paralleling the busy A4042 but generally following either sidewalks, cycleways or limited use streets. Magically NCR 88 becomes NCR 47 again just north of the remains of **Newport Castle** Ⓦ. It's a really complicated path as the route approaches the roundabout with the A4042, B4591 and Queensway but in a clever bit of design involving subway tunnels it continues uninterrupted and avoids street traffic. The route even skirts the castle for a closeup view.[4]

Continuing south from the castle NCR 47 follows the Kutaisi Walk along the bank of the Usk, passing the Riverfront Arts Centre, the Newport City Footbridge and the University of South Wales. Just a short distance from the river walk you'll also find the **Newport Museum and Art Gallery** Ⓦ.

*Newport Transporter Bridge*
*Credit: CC BY-SA 3.0 Tiia Monto*
`bit.ly/30lBLAs`

You could call it quits here because the footbridge about marks the end of what was the Monmouthshire Canal, but there are two other points of interest since you've come so far already.

NCR 47 continues past student housing and another bridge but finally ends in a "T" with NCR 4.[5] This intersection is about at what was the southern end of the original Town Docks.[6] There's still a large ship-shaped open area bounded by the Usk Road and East Dock Road.

---

4   The castle, which is in a precarious state, is protected by fencing. The 14th-century castle is best viewed from the nearby Newport Bridge and is an easy diversion by foot or bike. Sadly much of the castle has been obliterated by the bridge and another railway bridge.

5   NCR 4 to the west connects to Pembrokeshire and to the east Chepstow, Bristol, Bath, Reading and London

6   The Town Docks were filled in about 1930 in favor of the larger and still existing Alexandra Docks just south

The open area will probably disappear shortly because of planned development for Old Town Dock.

Continue west on NCR 4 for the last attraction of this trip. You'll follow the sidewalk on the A48 until arriving at the **Newport Transporter Bridge**. This bridge is more than a hundred years old and is one of the few transporter bridges left in existence. It's more of an aerial ferry than bridge. Cars (only a few at a time) enter a gondola suspended by cables from a high girder truss. The truss is held up by tall towers and the gondola is moved along the truss by electric motors.

Unfortunately these motors need repair so the gondola is presently not working although you can still climb the 270 steps up the towers and cross the river via the open metal grating. Well, some people can.

## Crumlin Arm

The Crumlin Arm was an 11mi/17.7km extension of the Monmouthshire Canal but today only about 7.7mi/12.3km remain visible. Short stretches are navigable, but the only narrowboats are trip boats operated by canal societies. NCR 47 and 465 follow the towpath all the way from Malpas to where the canal disappears under the A467 at Cwmcarn. This description might make it sound like it's not worth a walk or ride but it's a lovely stretch of canal.

From that roundabout at the M4 and A4051, the Crumlin Arm travels west southwest, at first hugging the south side of the M4. At Gwastad Lock No. 2, however, the canal gets some distance from the M4 before passing under the motorway and heading west. Gwastad Lock has been restored and the lock and bridge are quite attractive (I've seen some nice watercolors). There are six locks before the canal passes under the motorway.

On the other side of the M4 you'll find the Fourteen Locks or Cefn Flight. This impressive bit of engineering raises the canal 160ft/50m in just 800yd/740m. There's a complex system of weirs, sluices and side ponds that keep the closely spaced locks from overflowing. Five of the locks have been restored, beginning with the top lock just below the **Fourteen Locks Canal Centre**.

The canal centre has a tearoom, museum, art gallery, meeting space and toilets. And if you're lucky the canal trust trip boat might be traveling the locks although there's no set schedule. There's also a mini-market opposite the canal centre.

The flight is quite peculiar because there are five pairs of closely spaced locks, one group of three locks and the single top lock. The pairs are so closely spaced you'd think they were staircase locks—that is the bottom gate of one lock is the top gate of the next—but in fact there's a short distance (shorter than a boat length) between the pairs.

Another peculiarity is the mystery lock, number 11. It's in the middle of the group of three locks and has unexplained shelves of unequal depth on either side of the lock chamber. No one knows the purpose of these shelves or indeed even why the lock was built (it was added later).

 At the canal centre the towpath briefly coincides with the 26mi/42km **Sirhowy Valley Walk** ⓦ, which also meets the Ebbw Valley Walk at Crosskeys. The Sirhowy River meets the Ebbw River at Crosskeys.

After the canal centre the Crumlin Arm continues northwest through Rogerstone, passing homes but still shrouded by trees that guard the canal's serenity. Some of the advantages of passing through Rogerstone include the proximity of nearby pubs, cafés and grocery stores, all of which you'll find on the **online map** ⓦ.

Once the canal reaches the Newport Golf Club the country side opens up around the canal as it hugs the side of the Ebbw Valley. You'll have nice views of the valley from the canal, which still looks like a proper canal passing through a succession of original canal bridges. Unfortunately as the canal passes through Risca you'll find several culverts that make the canal unnavigable at Manor Road, Lower Wyndham Terrace/Thistle Way, Gelli Avenue and Navigation Road. The cycle route continues except for the need of street-level crossings.

Sandwiched between the Ebbw and the canal near Navigation Road you'll find the **Risca Industrial History Museum** ⓦ, which, though small, boasts a salvaged chemist's shop from Cardiff. Unfortunately it's only open on Saturdays. The museum is housed in the former Risca Collieries Workmens Hall and Miners Institute.

Again the benefit of the canal passing through this built-up area is an embarrassment of pubs and restaurants. In fact you'll find the Ebbw Valley is practically the vale of fish and chip shops.

There are rail stations at Rogerstone, Risca/Pontymister and Crosskeys convenient to the canal

The canal completely disappears for a short stretch after Navigation Road but when it reappears at Darren Road you'll come across **Whysom's Wharf Camping & Caravan Site and Tearooms** ⓦ and a summer trip boat operated by the **Islwyn Canal Association** ⓦ, a canal group I only learned of while researching this route.

After Risca the countryside again opens up as the canal hugs the sides of Medart, either a hill or mountain depending on your definition at 1,260ft/384m. It and the adjacent Twmbarlwm at 1,375ft/419m are distinctive landmarks of the Ebbw Valley.

 Just west of Whysom's Wharf NCR 47 splits with 47 continuing east to follow the Sirhowy River and NCR 467 going north to follow the canal to its end. Unfortunately there's no cycle route that would allow an easy ride to Crumlin. There's no evidence of Crumlin Wharf, which was the original terminus, but at some point after the creation of the staggering Crumlin Railway Viaduct, it ended about where the Viaduct Hotel (now a pub) is located. Sadly the viaduct was demolished in the late 1960s.

The mountains (or hills) north of the canal also provide excellent hiking and mountain biking opportunities. The Twrch Trail is 8.3mi/13.4km and climbs 1,443ft/440M with sections called Giant's Finger and Dragon's Teeth. Much too scary for me but Cwmcarn Forest also offers a lot of hiking trails as well as the nicest looking camp sites I've ever seen. There are pads for caravans, tents and even some glamping huts along with a café, gift shop, toilet, shower and laundry facilities. **Cwmcarn Forest Drive Camp Site** ⓦ would be an ideal location for exploring the canal as it's an easy ride to the end of the canal and the aforementioned Crosskeys station.

 Theoretically you can hire a mountain bike to be used on the Cwmcarn trails at **PS Cycles** ⓦ, but booking the bike at the website is problematic and it might be best to call.

If you're looking for more traditional lodging near the end of the canal you'll also find several B&Bs and **Cwmcarn Hotel** ⓦ. Well, the latter isn't exactly traditional as it offers bunk beds and secure lock up for cyclists.

The canal finally disappears where the B4591/Twyncarn Roads meets in a roundabout with the A467. Happily the "head" of the canal has been recently relined and improved, but it's still sad to think of the section of the canal that's forever lost under the roadway. If you do make it this far, take a few extra steps (100ft/30m) to contemplate the Flannel Factory Memorial Bench, which honors the 12 lives lost when a dam burst. The dam formed a reservoir to supply the Crumlin Arm but torrential rains in 1875 clogged the spillway and caused the embankment to fail, washing away the factory.

## Information

 Environment Agency rod license
bit.ly/2Y5rQhh

 Islwyn Canal Association
bit.ly/2N4V0w0

 Sirhowy Valley Walk
bit.ly/2RrRx9a

 Goytre Wharf
bit.ly/2Ja2lFc

 Pontypool Walk/Cycle map
bit.ly/31w8anZ

 Mon & Brec to Newpot map
bit.ly/2YHTghD

 Crumlin Arm map
bit.ly/2ZYat2M

## Attractions

 Ty Coch Lock Flight
bit.ly/2WW5OvN

 Fourteen Locks Canal Centre
bit.ly/2N2AUlL

 Pontymoile Marina
bit.ly/2L7Pwhf

 Newport Transporter Bridge
bit.ly/2XuTQhg

 Newport Museum and Art Gallery
bit.ly/31L4v6B

 Risca Industrial History Museum
bit.ly/2WUG96J

 Newport Castle
bit.ly/2RuREAS

 Pontypool Folly
bit.ly/2YB0zaC

 Pontypool Park
bit.ly/2Fs71oZ

## Hotels

*Pontypool*

 Premier Inn
bit.ly/2WXm93v

 Best Western Metro
bit.ly/31NUHsu

*Cwmcarn*

 Cwmcarn Hotel
bit.ly/2KXWOm6

## Transportation

 Pontypool & New Inn station
bit.ly/2KvRxEr

Watkin Taxi
1873 881012

Martyns Taxi Cwmbran
7807 368414

Alex Taxis
7733 323316

## B&Bs

 Oriel Garn
bit.ly/2LeuopP

 Ty-Cooke Farm B&B
bit.ly/2Ku9SC1

## Dining

*Goytre/Penperlleni*

 The Goytre Arms
bit.ly/31QSJYk

 Goytre Fish Bar & Tandoori
bit.ly/2KuGoUp

 The Horseshoe Inn
bit.ly/2KwLjUL

 The Star Inn
bit.ly/2IYKxwJ

*Pontypool*

 The Horse & Jockey
bit.ly/2XVzbDn

*Sebastopol*

 The Open
Hearth
bit.ly/2KwmAA5

*Cwmbran*

 The Old
Bridgend Inn
bit.ly/2L9CKyP

 The
Waterloo
bit.ly/2Fq4iMC

## Fish & chips

 Pontnewydd
Fish Bar
bit.ly/2RDctKF

 Page's Fish
& Chips
bit.ly/2x8u4Av

## Café

 The Lock
Cafe
bit.ly/2J6G8Yu

## Camping

*Crumlin Arm*

 Whysom's Wharf
Camping&Tearooms
bit.ly/2x7qlTX

 Cwmcarn Forest
Drive Camp Site
bit.ly/2L7bMry

## Groceries/Cafe

*Cwmbran*

 ALDI
bit.ly/2Ky4aiy

 Sainsbury's
bit.ly/2L9taw0

 Lidl
bit.ly/2ZcF93l

 Asda
bit.ly/2RsJ5GJ

## Bikes

 PS Cycles
(Cwmcarn)
bit.ly/2WZYcbG

## Misc

 Lloyd's Pharmacy
(Cwmbran)
bit.ly/2ZG4IWO

*Another common sight on the canal are these benches that show the path of the canal from Brecon to Newport, including the Crumlin Arm*

# Conclusion

It's a little silly to offer a conclusion to this guide because your enjoyment of the Monmouthshire & Brecon Canal will stay with you long after you read this guide and long after you take your trip on the canal. It's very likely the effects of the trip will be lasting and potentially habit forming. In odd moments, perhaps while stuck in traffic or in a boring meeting at work, you'll find yourself back on the canal.

You'll remember that curry you ate that belies the British reputation for bland food or that cream tea that made a satisfying reward for an arduous day of shopping. You'll find that you've bored your friends to death with your photos of aqueducts, locks and countless herons. You'll find yourself planning your next canal trip, or even contemplating a return to the Mon & Brec to address those ruins, standing stones, quaint villages or historical markers you missed the first time.

## Apologies

In fact I really should have labeled this chapter "Apologies," especially if this is or will be your first canal trip. You're now hopelessly doomed to a future of frustration as you try to explain to your friends just how unbelievable, super cool, stupendous and amazing your trip was. You'll have to experience blank stares as you explain your two-and-a-half mile an hour trip, standing at the tiller in the rain, hoping you make it to the pub before lunch service ends. Or the night you spent in the boat with no internet service, no television and only the conversation of your loved ones and friends—perhaps bolstered by alcohol beverages and cold takeway fish and chips—to occupy the time.

This has certainly been my burden since my first narrowboat trip on the Kennet & Avon Canal. Since then I've traveled by boat and/or bike the Llangollen, Montgomery, Worcester & Birmingham, Birmingham & Fazeley, Stratford Upon Avon and Droitwich canals. So perhaps you should look at this book as a curse, forever condemning you to forgo other trips unless it involve a canal.

Well, I think you'll forgive me for settling this burden on you. If you want to vent your frustration, feel free to visit my website or facebook page. I'd love to hear how I've ruined your life.

 Narrowboatingfor
Beginners.com
bit.ly/2OKJHde

 Narrowboating for
Beginners at facebook
bit.ly/2M6AidU

*Approaching the Ashford Tunnel, the only tunnel on the CRT maintained canal
Credit: James Bates*

# Appendix

## Bridges / aqueducts / locks

Bridges, aqueducts and locks are the most reliable guides to your progress on the canal. Most of the original mile markers have been stolen and those that remain are on the towpath and not visible from the water. Most bridges have names although sometimes it's just the name of the road or nearby farm. Only bridge numbers are displayed. Not all bridges are numbered. Some numbers are missing as bridges have been removed. The highest numbered bridges are in Brecon. Numbering continues south on the unnavigable Monmouthshire Canal. Bridges (and the Ashford Tunnel) in bold indicate a low clearance.

Assume most locks and lift bridges will take 15–20 minutes to negotiate, although obviously that changes depending on traffic.

| No. | Name | Dist. to Brecon mi/km | Dist. to end* mi/km | No. | Name | Dist. to Brecon mi/km | Dist. to end* mi/km |
|---|---|---|---|---|---|---|---|
| 167 | Dadford's Bridge | 224/73.8[†] | 34.7/55.9 | 150 | Penawr Lift Bridge | 5.7/9.2 | 29.1/46.8 |
| 166 | Gas Works Bridge | 549/167.3[†] | 34.7/55.8 | 149 | Gethinog Lift Bridge | 5.8/9.4 | 29/46.6 |
| 165 | The Watton Bridge | 0.4/0.6 | 34.4/55.4 | 148 | Draw Bridge | 5.9/9.6 | 28.8/46.4 |
| 165A | Brecon Flyover | 1.3/2.1 | 33.5/53.9 | 147 | Cross Oak Bridge | 6.1/9.9 | 28.6/46.1 |
| 164 | Brynich Bridge | 1.5/2.4 | 33.3/53.6 | 146 | Chilson Bridge | 6.6/10.6 | 28.2/45.4 |
| 1 | Cefn Brynich Aqueduct | 1.5/2.4 | 33.3/53.5 | 145 | Beniah Bridge | 6.7/10.8 | 28.1/45.2 |
| 69 | Brynich Lock | 2.1/3.4 | 32.7/52.6 | 144 | Talybont Draw Bridge | 6.9/11.1 | 27.9/44.9 |
| 163 | Cefn Brynich Bridge | " " | " " | 4 | Aqueduct | 7.0/11.3 | 27.7/44.6 |
| 2 | Usk Aqueduct | 2.3/3.6 | 32.5/52.3 | 143 | White Hart Bridge | 7.1/11.4 | 27.7/44.6 |
| 162 | Brynich Turn Bridge | 2.4/3.8 | 32.4/52.2 | | Talybont Railway Bridge | 7.1/11.4 | 27.7/44.5 |
| 161 | Bell Ear Bridge | 2.6/4.2 | 32.2/51.8 | 142 | Graig-Las Bridge | 7.3/11.7 | 27.5/44.2 |
| 160 | Ty-Newydd Bridge No. 2 | 3.2/5.1 | 31.6/50.8 | | **Ashford Tunnel** | 7.8/12.6 | 26.8/43.1 |
| 159 | Ty-Newydd Bridge | 3.4/5.4 | 31.4/50.5 | 141 | Upper Wenallt Bridge | 8.2/13.3 | 26.5/42.7 |
| 158 | Storehouse Bridge | 3.5/5.6 | 31.3/50.3 | 140 | Lower Wenallt Bridge | 8.4/13.6 | 26.3/42.4 |
| 3 | Aqueduct | 3.7/5.9 | 31.1/50 | 139A | **Snake Bridge** | 8.5/13.8 | 26.2/42.2 |
| 157 | Llan-Brynean Bridge | 3.9/6.3 | 30.9/49.7 | 139 | Llandetty Bridge | 8.6/13.9 | 26.1/42.1 |
| 156 | Low Bridge | 4.3/7 | 30.4/49 | 138 | Parsons Bridge | 9/14.5 | 25.8/41.5 |
| 155 | Court Farm Lift Bridge | 4.6/7.5 | 30.1/48.5 | 137 | Dan-Y-Graig Bridge | 9.3/14.9 | 25.5/41.1 |
| 154 | Pencelli Bridge | 4.7/7.6 | 30/48.4 | 136 | Workhouse Bridge | 9.4/15.2 | 25.3/40.7 |
| 153 | Cross Keys Bridge | 4.8/7.8 | 29.9/48.2 | 135 | Toffs Lock Bridge | 9.7/15.5 | 25.1/40.4 |
| 152 | Castle Bridge | 5.0/8.1 | 29.7/47.9 | 68 | Toffs Lock (top lock) | 9.7/15.7 | 25/40.3 |
| 151 | Penawr Bridge | 5.5/8.9 | 29.2/47 | 67 | Little Lock | 9.8/15.7 | 25/40.2 |

*    Distance to end of CRT control, just south of Solomon's bridge
†    Distance in feet and meters
‡    Very sharp turn

# The Monmouthshire & Brecon Canal

| No. | Name | Dist. to Brecon mi/km | Dist. to end* mi/km |
|---|---|---|---|
| 66 | Gwlawcoed Lock | 9.8/15.8 | 24.9/40.1 |
| 134 | Coombes Lock Bridge | 10.1/16.2 | 24.7/39.8 |
| 65 | Coombes (aka Depot) Lock | " " | 24.7/39.7 |
| 5 | Aqueduct | " " | 24.6/39.6 |
| 133 | Coach & Horses Bridge | 10.3/16.6 | 24.5/39.5 |
| 64 | Lower Lock (bottom lock) | 10.4/16.7 | 24.4/39.3 |
| 132 | Lower Lock Bridge | " " | " " |
| 131 | Yard Bridge | 10.7/17.2 | 24.1/39.8 |
| 130 | Aberyail Bridge | 11.1/17.9 | 23.7/38.1 |
| 129 | Panteague Bridge | 11.3/18.2 | 23.4/37.7 |
| 6 | Claisfer Aqueduct | 11.4/18.3 | 23.3/37.6 |
| 128 | **Panteague Bridge** | 11.5/18.5 | 23.2/37.4 |
| 127 | Old House Bridge | 11.8/19 | 23/37 |
| 126 | Aberhowie Bridge | 12/19.3 | 22.7/36.6 |
| 125 | Dyfnant Bridge | 12.4/19.9 | 22.4/36 |
| 124 | Spiteful Inn Bridge | 12.7/20.4 | 22.1/35.3 |
| 123 | Pen-Y-Bryn Bridge | 12.9/20.8 | 21.9/35.3 |
| 122 | **The Fro Bridge** | 13.1/21.1 | 21.7/34.9 |
| 121A | Glan Usk Bridge | 13.4/21.6 | 21.4/34.4 |
| 121 | Llwyncelyn Bridge | 13.6/21.9 | 21.2/34 |
| 120 | Baylis Bridge | 13.8/22.2 | 21/33.8 |
| 119 | Folly Bridge | 14.4/23.2 | 20.4/32.9 |
| 118 | Workhouse Bridge | 14.6/23.5 | 20.1/32.4 |
| 117 | Dan-Y-Garth Bridge | 14.9/24 | 19.9/32 |
| 116 | Ffawyddog Bridge | 15/24.1 | 19.8/31.8 |
| 7 | Aqueduct | 15.3/24.6 | 19.4/31.3 |
| 115 | Upper Yard Bridge | 15.4/24.8 | 19.4/31.2 |
| 114 | Lower Yard Bridge | 15.5/24.9 | 19.3/31 |
| 113 | Llwmws Bridge | 15.9/25.6 | 18.9/30.4 |
| 112 | Park Bridge | 16.1/25.9 | 18.7/30 |
| 111 | Wooden Bridge | 16.3/26.2 | 18.5/29.7 |
| 110 | Pen-Pedair-Heol Bridge | 16.4/26.4 | 18.3/29.5 |
| 109 | Dan-Y-Parc Bridge | 16.7/26.9 | 18.1/29.1 |
| 107 | Dan-Y-Graig Bridge | 17.6/28.3 | 17.2/27.6 |
| 106 | Ffynnon-Yr-Eirin Bridge | 18/29 | 16.8/27 |
| 105 | Sand Bridge | 18.3/29.4 | 16.5/27.6 |
| 104 | Auckland Bridge | 18.5/29.8 | 16.2/26.1 |
| 8 | Aqueduct | 18.6/29.9 | 16.1/26 |
| 9 | Aqueduct | 18.7/30.1 | " " |
| 103 | **Navigation Bridge** | 18.8/30.2 | 16/25.7 |
| 102 | Ty-Gwynn Bridge | 19.3/31.1 | 15.5/24.9 |
|  | Heads Of The Valleys Bridge | " " | 15.4/24.9 |
| 101 | Heol-Yr-Allt Bridge | 19.5/31.4 | 15.2/24.5 |
| 100 | **Humphrey's Bridge** | 19.8/31.9 | 14.9/24 |
| 99 | Llanwenarth Bridge | 19.9/32 | 14.8/23.9 |
| 10 | Church Road Aqueduct | 20.1/32.3 | 14.7/23.6 |
| 11 | Cwm Shenkin Brook Aqduct | 20.2/32.5 | 14.5/23.4 |
| 98 | (Station Rd) Bridge | 20.4/32.8 | 14.4/23.2 |
| 97A | Railway Bridge | 20.5/33 | 14.2/22.9 |
| 97 | Govilon Yard Bridge | 20.7/33.3 | 14/22.6 |
| 96 | Govilon Turn Bridge | 21/33.8 | 13.8/22.2 |
| 12 | Aqueduct | 21.4/34.4 | 13.4/21.6 |
| 12A | Aqueduct | 21.8/35.1 | 12.9/20.8 |
| 95A | **Tod's Bridge** ‡ | 21.9/35.2 | " " |
| 95 | Castle Upper Bridge | 22.4/36 | 12.3/19.9 |
| 94 | Castle Lower Bridge | 22.6/36.4 | 12.1/19.5 |
| 13 | Aqueduct | 22.9/36.8 | 11.9/19.2 |
| 93 | (Bridge Farm) Bridge | 23.1/37.2 | 11.7/18.9 |
| 92 | Heol Gerrig Bridge | 23.5/37.8 | 11.3/18.2 |
| 91 | Wooden Bridge | 23.7/38.1 | 11.1/17.8 |
| 90 | Morgan's Bridge | 23.9/38.5 | 10.9/17.6 |
| 89 | Barn Bridge | 24.2/38.9 | 10.6/17 |
| 88 | Twynglas Bridge | 24.3/39.1 | 10.5/16.9 |
| 87 | Poplar Bridge | 24.5/39.4 | 10.3/16.6 |
| 86 | Ochram Turn Bridge | 24.6/35.6 | 10.2/16.4 |
| 14 | Ochram Turn Aqueduct | 24.7/39.7 | 10.1/16.2 |
| 85 | Thimbles Bridge | 25/40.2 | 9.8/15.7 |
| 84 | Ty-Coch Bridge | 25.2/40.5 | 9.6/15.5 |
| 83 | Beech Tree Bridge | 25.4/40.9 | 9.4/15.1 |
| 82 | Pwllyrhwyaid Bridge | 25.6/41.3 | 9.1/14.7 |
| 81 | Llanover Bridge | 25.7/41.4 | 9/14.5 |
| 80 | **Mount Pleasant Upper Br** | 25.9/41.7 | 8.9/14.3 |
| 79 | Lower Mount Pleasant Bridge | 26.1/42 | 8.7/14 |
| 14A | Mill Turn Aqueduct | 26.4/42.4 | 8.4/13.5 |
| 78 | Mill Turn Bridge | 26.4/42.6 | 8.3/13.4 |
| 77 | Cottage Bridge | 26.8/43.2 | 8/12.8 |
| 76 | Lapstone Bridge | 26.9/43.3 | 7.9/12.6 |
| 75 | Jenkin Rosser Bridge | 27.2/43.8 | 7.5/12.1 |
| 15 | Goytre Aqueduct | 27.5/44.2 | 7.3/11.7 |
| 74 | Saron Bridge | 27.8/44.8 | 6.9/11.2 |
| 73 | Penrehoel Bridge | 28/45.1 | 6.7/10.9 |
| 72 | Parc-Y-Brain Bridge | 28.3/45.6 | 6.5/10.4 |
| 71 | Lower Parc-Y-Brain Bridge | 28.4/45.7 | 6.4/10.3 |
| 70 | Birdspool Bridge | 28.8/46.4 | 6/9.6 |

| No. | Name | Dist. to Brecon mi/km | Dist. to end* mi/km |
|---|---|---|---|
| 69 | High House Bridge | 29/46.7 | 5.8/9.3 |
| 68 | Croes-Y-Pant Bridge | 29.2/47.1 | 5.5/8.9 |
| 67 | Pentre Bridge | 29.4/47.4 | 5.3/8.6 |
| 66 | Brook Farm Bridge | 29.7/47.7 | 5.1/8.2 |
| 65 | Mortimer's Bridge | 29.8/48 | 4.9/7.9 |
| 64 | Skinner's Bridge | 30/48.2 | 4.8/7.7 |
| 63 | Mamhilad Bridge | 30.1/48.5 | 4.6/7.4 |
| 62 | High Bridge | 30.5/49.1 | 4.2/6.8 |
| 61 | Troed-Y-Rhiw Bridge | 30.8/49.6 | 3.9/6.3 |
| 60 | Govera Bridge | 31/49.9 | 3.8/6 |
| 59 | Keepers Bridge | 31.1/50.1 | 3.6/5.8 |
| 58 | Upper Wern Bridge | 31.4/50.6 | 3.3/5.4 |
| 57 | Lower Wern Bridge | 31.6/50.9 | 3.1/5.1 |
| 56 | Squires Bridge | 32.3/52 | 2.4/3.9 |

| No. | Name | Dist. to Brecon mi/km | Dist. to end* mi/km |
|---|---|---|---|
| 55 | **Jockey Bridge** | 32.5/52.2 | 2.3/3.7 |
| 53 | Pontypool Rd Bridge | 33/53.1 | 1.8/2.9 |
| 16 | Aqueduct | 33.1/53.3 | 1.7/2.7 |
| 17 | Aqueduct | "" | 1.6/2.5 |
| 18 | Aqueduct | 33.2/53.4 | "" |
| 52 | Pontymoile Bridge | 33.3/53.5 | 1.5/2.4 |
| 51A | Pontymoile Flyover Bridge | "" | "" |
| 51 | Coed-Y-Gric Bridge | 33.5/53.9 | 1.3/2.1 |
| 50A | Railway Viaduct | "" | "" |
| 50 | Union Bridge | 33.7/54.3 | 1.0/1.7 |
| 49 | **Panteg Bridge** | 34.1/54.8 | 0.7/1.1 |
| 48 | Crown Bridge | 34.5/55.6 | 0.2/0.4 |
| 47 | Solomon's Bridge | 34.7/55.9 | 191/58.2† |

# How to pronounce Welsh place names

Unfortunately trying to pronounce Welsh is a near impossible task despite the rules for pronunciation being fairly straight forward. After all, advice like being told every letter of a word is pronounced doesn't help when there are *so* many letters and *so* many are pronounced differently from English.

What does help, especially with place names, is that many words use the same building blocks. So once you've learned how to pronounce "llan" half the battle is won.

By the way, I'm sure my pronunciation guide is laughable and any Welsh speaker will cringe at my advice. Further, this guide is a compilation of several sources, many of which conflict. And even though it's a small country, there are regional differences between north, south and middle.

## Consonants

- "C" is always hard like "K", as in "car"
- "CH" sounds like the hushed sound in the Scottish "loch" or how pretentious people say the name of a German composer
- "D" by itself sounds no different but "DD" sounds like "th" as in "thought"
- "F" by itself sounds like the "V" sound in "love", but "FF" sounds like a regular "F"
- "G" is hard like "get"
- "L" by itself sounds no different, but "LL" sounds like "thl." It's like making the "L" sound of "love" while blowing air on either side of your tongue—at the risk of

looking like Harpo Marx
- "RH" is pronounced as if the "H" came first

## Vowels

- There's nothing special about "A," "E" and "O" but "I" sounds like "ee" as in "queen"
- "U" usually sounds like the "i" in "sit" but if it ends a word like the "ee" in "queen." So the Welsh word for Wales, Cymru, is pronounced "cum-REE," but the numeral 5 spelled "pump" is pronounced "pimp" (but with an almost silent last "p").
- W sounds like the "oo" in "zoom." So Cwmbran comes out as "COOM-bran." Unless, of course, "W" is next to another vowel, in which case it sounds like a regular "W." So "Gwynedd" is pronounced "GWIN-eth."

- "Rs" are rolled just once. Try not to sound like a comic Scot

- Y will drive you nuts. In the last syllable of a word it's a soft "i" sound but otherwise it's like the "U" in "fun." So the Welsh word for mountain—"mynydd"— sounds like "MUN-ith." If "Y" appears as the definite article it's pronounced "uh."
- Adding a circumflex or "^" above a vowel as in "glân" lengthens the vowel and will change the meaning of the same word without the circumflex. So "glân" pronounced "GLANE" means to clean but "glan" pronounced how it looks means riverbank or shore.

Another big aid in pronouncing Welsh is that generally the accent is on the penultimate syllable.

## Building blocks

- "Llan" seems to start half the place names on the canal, but that's because "llan," pronounced "thlan," refers to the land owned by a religious group like a monastic order. "Llan" is then followed by the name of a saint, so the church at Llangynidr (thlan-gun-NEE-dur) was dedicated to Saints Mary and Cynidr. (And although the penultimate syllable is accented, it's mild.)
- "Pont," pronounced as it looks, is very common in place names

along canals because it means bridge, and "camlas" means "canal"
- "Aber" means mouth of a river and "afon," pronounced "avon," means river, so yes the River Avon means the River River. It also explains why there are so many River Avons in the UK.
- "Newydd" or "NEW-ith" means new
- "Ysgol" or "US-gol" means school
- "Caer" or "CARE" means fort
- "Cefn" or "KEV-en" means ridge

## Pronunciation guides

 Welsh
place names
bit.ly/2LkV3kN

 Cycle
Wales
bit.ly/2ZQvwnl

 Ordnance Survey
Welsh guide
bit.ly/31XB5CB

 Go 4
a walk
bit.ly/2XbbxTK

- "Cwm" and "pant" both mean valley
- "Bach" and "fach" can both mean little or small but "Tŷ bach" can mean toilet—literally "little room." Or just say toilet because "toiled" is also Welsh for toilet.
- "Nant" is brook or creek

## Useful phrases

- "Croeso" or "CROY-saw" means "welcome"
- Thankfully "hello" works just fine in Welsh but "goodbye" is "hwyl" or "WHO-ill." "Hwyl fawr" means "all the best."[1]
- "Bore da" means "good day," but you will want to pronounce the "E" as an "eh" sound
- "Prynhawn da" or "PRIN-hown dah" means good afternoon. Often shortened to "P'nown dah"
- "Noswaith dda" or good evening mildly violates the pronounce every letter rule and comes out "NOS-waith ah," so the two "th" sounds become one
- "Nos da" or "NOS dah" is good night
- "Diolch" is thank you and sounds like "DEE-olchhh"
- Finally the least useful phrase is "Ydych chi'n siarad Saesneg?" or "Do you speak English?" This phrase is useless because I've yet to meet a non-English speaker in Wales and because it's so difficult to say this. The closest I can come to this is "Uh dach kin SHAH-red SIZE-neg?"

# Mooring

The usual mooring rules apply to the Mon & Brec: You can moor overnight anywhere along the towpath except near bridges, locks or anywhere you're told not to moor. You can moor for 14 days unless informed otherwise. Of course you can moor next to a lock or lift bridge while you're waiting or preparing to turn the lock or lift the bridge but

1  If you're female you'll sound like a native if you greet people with a cheery "hiya." However, it seemed to me that there's always a note of concern in this greeting, as if talking to daft person or a lost child. Of course it might just be the other person recognizes me as an American.

you should avoid blocking other boats trying to do the same thing. And in general you shouldn't moor where your boat would block navigation such as at a sharp bend.

When mooring at services such as waterpoints avoid mooring any longer than it takes to accomplish your task. On the Mon & Brec, avoid mooring at the green charging stations for Castle Narrowboats, unless you're charging a boat.

| Location | Duration | Location | Duration |
|---|---|---|---|
| Brecon Terminus | 24 hours | Govilon Wharf | 14 days |
| Bridge 142 Talybont-on-Usk | 14 days | Goytre Wharf | 48 hours |
| Lock 65 Llangynidr | 14 days | Pontymoile Basin | 14 days |
| Llangattock | 48 hours | Bridge 45 (Five Locks Basin) | 48 hours |
| Gilwern Wharf | 14 days | | |

## Services

♦♦ Toilets  Showers  Elsan disposal  Rubbish  Waterpoint  Sewage pump out  Slipway

| Location | Services | Location | Services |
|---|---|---|---|
| Bridge 166 Brecon | | Govilon Wharf | |
| Bridge 142 Talybont-on-Usk | | Goytre Wharf | |
| Lock 65 Llangynidr | | Pontymoile Basin | |
| Bridge 115 Llangattock | | Bridge 45 (Five Locks Basin) | |
| Gilwern Wharf | | | |

# About the author

I'm the author of *Narrowboating for Beginners: What Americans need to know when considering a narrowboat vacation in the UK* and *Cycling the Canals of Britain: The Adventures of a Solitary Cyclist*. I've also written mysteries and science fiction and have several books in the works.

Next year I'll start writing a guide to the Kennet & Avon Canal as well as the third edition of *Narrowboating for Beginners*.

## Kindle version

If you bought this guide at a bookstore instead of through Amazon, then thank you for supporting your local bookstore. Unfortunately that support means that you didn't automatically get the Kindle edition of the book with your purchase, but if you send me an email with a photograph of the cover (with you in the picture and not obviously standing in a bookstore), then I will send you a link to download the Kindle file.

> Send an email to: info@narrowboatingforbeginners.com
> and make the subject: Mon & Brec Guide Kindle version

You might also specify whether you want the replica Kindle edition, which is an exact reproduction of the print edition, or a reflowable text version that allows you to change the typeface and font size.

I'd also love to hear about your narrowboat trip and any suggestions how I might improve the next edition.

## Corrections

One of the advantages to self-publishing is that I can make additions or corrections quite easily. So if you've found an error or want to be included in the guide, just send me an email with the subject Mon & Brec Guide update.

 Of course if you've bought a paperback copy, it won't magically update, but you can find any updates or corrections to my canal books at my website: bit.ly/2p5LWvm

 Your Kindle version can be updated, but unless it's a major revision you won't be automatically notified of updates. You can periodically update your copy by visiting Amazon's manage your content page: amzn.to/2iwCn3u

If you have an EPUB edition of the book, it may be difficult to know when the book has updated, so check the corrections pages and if you'd like an updated EPUB

Send an email to info@narrowboatingforbeginners.com and make the subject: Mon & Brec Guide EPUB update

Printed in Great Britain
by Amazon

66847304R00078